SCRIPOPHILY
The Art of Finance

Keith Hollender

Museum of American Financial History. 26 Broadway, Room 200, New York, NY 10004-1763

ACKNOWLEDGEMENTS

In addition to the invaluable information drawn from the publications listed in the bibliography, particular thanks are due to Edward Swan for his assistance on early share trading, Michael Veissid and Howard Shakespeare for their factual contributions across a range of subjects, Jörg Benecke for help on German material, the International Bond & Share Society and the Museum of American Financial History for access to published and research material. Thanks are also due to those who either provided photographs or loaned original items from their collections for the many illustrations. These include the Museum of American Financial History, Sotheby's, Phillips, Herzog Hollender Phillips & Co, Scripophily International Promotions, Andrew Kirk, Jonathan Lyttleton, Howard Shakespeare and R. M. Smythe & Co. Proof reading and grammar corrections, of which there were many, were kindly done by John Herzog and my wife Veronica who have read this book far more times than they may care to remember! Pauline Snell provided frequent and generous advice on how to work the computer, a constant problem of modern technology.

© Museum of American Financial History and Questlook Ltd. 1994

Published in USA in 1994 by Museum of American Financial History
26 Broadway, New York, NY10004

All Rights Reserved.
No part of this publication may be reproduced, stored in a retrieval system, or transmitted, in any form or by any means, electronic, mechanical, photocopying, recording, or otherwise, without the prior permission of the Copyright owners.

Printed and bound in Great Britain by
Acanthus Press Ltd., Wellington, Somerset

Library of Congress Catalog Card Number: 94-78893

    Hollender, Keith
      Scripophily — The Art of Finance
      Bibliography: p.
      1. Stock certificates — Collectors and collecting
      2. Bonds — Collectors and collecting. I. Title
      ISBN 0-96426-300-9

SCRIPOPHILY
✣ The Art of Finance ✣

Few share certificates can match Compagnie des Maritimes de Bruges for design and colour.

CONTENTS

Introduction 7

PART 1 *General Background and History*
- The development of Scripophily 9
- What are bonds and shares? 10
- Printing and Engraving 18
- Art for Money's Sake 23
- Shares of History 26

PART 2 *Collecting Themes*
- Introduction 31

  Countries
  - Australia 32
  - Canada 34
  - China 38
  - France 46
  - Germany 51
  - Belgium 54
  - Holland 55
  - Great Britain 58
  - Russia 62
  - South Africa 72
  - Central & South America 76
  - United States of America 80
  - Other Countries

  Subjects
  - Early Material 88
  - Railways 93
  - Automobiles 106
  - Signatures 111
  - Mining 116
  - Banking 121
  - Shipping 129
  - Some Other Themes 133

PART 3 *Developing a Collection*
- What to look for and what to avoid 138
- Looking after a Collection 143
- How and Where to Sell 146

Appendices 152

Dealers, Auction Houses and Societies 152

Bibliography 154

Index 156

One would have thought there were more subtle ways of persuading the public to invest in Roumanian debt than by picturing the Transylvanian castle of Vlad the Impaler! The castle is reputed to have been the model for Bram Stoker's Dracula. But there again, the bond was issued in 1929, the year of the Great Crash.

"SCRIPOPHILY   THE ART OF FINANCE"

INTRODUCTION

Well over ten years have passed since publication of the first general introduction to the subject, "Scripophily — Collecting Bonds & Share Certificates". During that period the hobby has grown enormously. There are now estimated to be in the region of 100,000 collectors or "dabblers" in the field, some 200 dealers and 20-30 auction houses scattered across the world. Scripophily is firmly on the map, appealing not only to collectors but also to students of financial history or simply those looking for an attractive or amusing decoration. Not only has interest increased, but events have taken place changing and developing the whole field. Chinese and Russian bonds have reduced in number as a result of settlements and the market has expanded to cover every country in the world. Enormous national interest in German and American material has led to the creation of large and thriving markets in those countries (and others) with collectors eager to research their specialised fields.

This book builds on the original, covering the interim events and drawing from more recent detailed research.

The constant search for knowledge has led to the formation of several dedicated research institutions. History of finance is one area which has lagged behind more traditional historical avenues, but the formation of the Museum of American Financial History is a major step towards the coordination of financial research. To many, finance may seem a relatively new subject providing employment for the young and gifted and excuses for politicians to impose taxes. In fact the history of finance goes back almost 6,000 years to the beginnings of trade in the Near East. Evidence suggests that writing was invented and first used to monitor business transactions and it may come as a surprise to new and old scripophilists to know that the earliest bearer bonds date from 1700 BC!

So far as "Scripophily" is concerned it is not the intention here to travel so far back in time; this book is concerned with the more recent past (a mere 300 years). It is designed to introduce the newcomer to the hobby as well as enthuse existing collectors. It aims to cover a wide range of collecting themes and provide some historical background to those fascinating documents known as "stocks and bonds".

The book has been split into three main sections: General Background and History, Collecting Themes, and Developing a Collection. The appendices provide additional information on dealers, auction houses, reading material and societies.

One early word of advice: collecting simply for investment is best left to the experts and, although it is the intention to provide expert knowledge to the scripophilist, collecting for investment is not its prime message. Those deciding to start a collection should do so because of a personal interest in the subject itself and if, after a number of years, for reasons of rarity and demand, that collection acquires a premium value, then that is a bonus and not a justification of the original decision. Of course it is an undeniable fact that items genuinely produced in a past age are irreplaceable no matter how much modern technology develops. Many of these items get lost or destroyed as time moves on and an increasing number of people have the desire to collect such pieces of history — the result inevitably tends to be an excess of demand over supply.

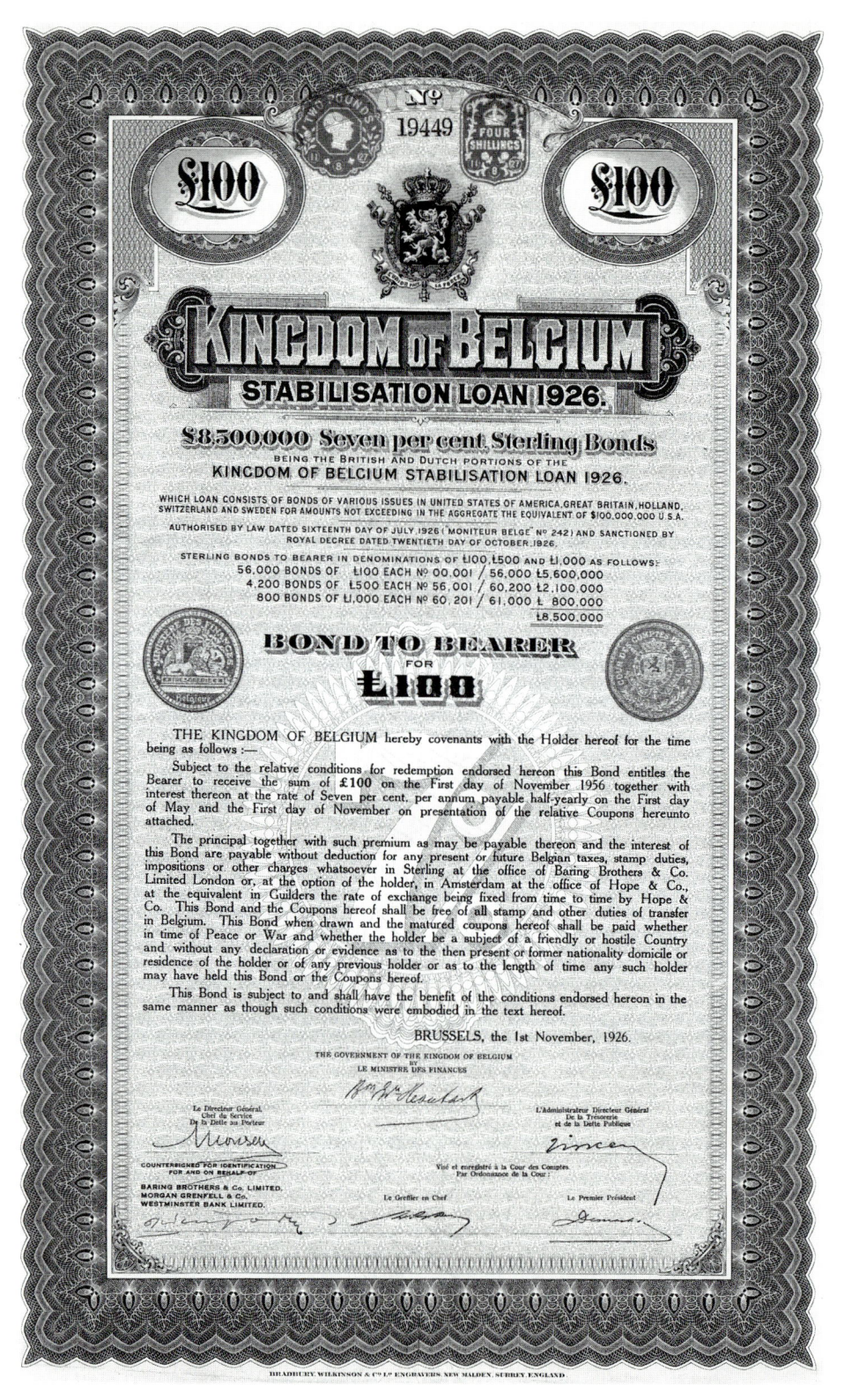

Just occasionally "live" bonds appear in the collectors market. Such items like this £100 bond of the Kingdom of Belgium escaped encashment but are still valid on surrender.

PART 1

General background and history

THE DEVELOPMENT OF SCRIPOPHILY

For years stockbrokers (or disappointed investors) accumulated attractive certificates at random. Some became lampshades and others were stored in drawers or attics "just in case". But Scripophily only began in earnest following the publication in 1976 of two catalogues in Germany listing and illustrating bonds issued by pre-revolutionary China and Russia. The catalogues were the result of doctoral research by two German bankers, Ulrich Drumm and Alfons Henseler.

Some two years later following the formation of the Bond & Share Society and the emergence of specialist dealers, the market got under way. Initially centred in England, early activity was concentrated on Chinese and Russian bonds which since their default had maintained a quotation on the London Stock Exchange. Prices in the collector market moved and matched those on the Exchange and inevitably a speculative interest developed which tended to over-ride the intrinsic qualities of the certificates themselves. Three years of frenetic activity and dramatic price rises were followed by a sharp market correction but by 1982, the publication year of this book's first edition, scripophily was truly born — euphoria, birth pains and all.

LATER PROGRESS

Since 1982 the number of collectors has grown considerably in all parts of the world. This growth continues but still falls well short of the estimated 15-20 million stamp collectors or the many millions of banknote, coin, map and medal collectors. It is this enormous potential which many new collectors find so fascinating. From an initial base of around 300 collectors, estimates now put the figure at over 100,000. This increase has been achieved over only fifteen years and has been accompanied and encouraged by the establishment of many new dealers, auctions and local collectors' societies throughout the world stretching from New York to Australia. A list of major dealers and societies is given on page 152.

The number of publications, both books and magazines, has also increased and several are listed on page 153. But, perhaps of all the reasons for the growth, the most important has been the broadening of the field. No longer do Chinese and Russian bonds dominate the market. The establishment of the hobby in a wide range of countries has naturally led to the growth of local preferences; thus Swiss material is in great demand in Switzerland, early German shares in Germany, Palestine material in the Jewish community, Australian shares in Australia, and so on.

Apart from these localized biases, certain other sectors have risen to rank with China and Russia as "internationally" acceptable. The most notable of these is US Railroads. A vast field covering over 9,000 different companies and a time span of over one hundred and fifty years, both share certificates and bonds are extremely attractive, often with vignettes of early trains, stations and the occasional American Indian. The railroads were a major factor in the economic development of the United States and, consequently, it is not surprising that it is this sector which has become especially popular both in America and across the World.

As research goes on, scripophily develops. Still at an early stage in its life cycle, collectors can not only look forward to exciting advances over the coming years but more importantly can participate in that progress.

WHAT ARE BONDS AND SHARES?

Most bonds and shares collected today were, at one time or another, quoted on a stock market, whether London, Paris, New York or elsewhere. In the normal course of their life bonds would have been redeemed or cancelled and largely destroyed. Some, such as those issued by US Railroad companies, may have been assumed by other companies through takeover or merger before the end of their intended life, but others were defaulted. A default occurs when the borrower (government or company) fails to meet interest payments and ceases bond redemption. The act of default may not necessarily result in the removal of a stock exchange quotation as it is always hoped that the position will be corrected in the future. Over time several countries or states, legal or otherwise, defaulted on their bonds, thus creating much of the basic scrip of scripophily. Major defaults are summarised in the table below:

MAJOR INTERNATIONAL DEFAULTS

Country/State	Approximate amount defaulted
China	£60 million (c. $90 million)
Russia	Over £1 billion ($1.5 billion)
Confederates States of America	$712 million
Mexico	$12 million
State of Mississippi	$7 million

Outstanding debt of the Kingdom of Bulgaria was settled in 1987 and British holders of sterling bonds such as this received 40% of the face value. Many were handed in, some of which have mysteriously resurfaced overstamped "cancelled".

This list is far from complete and not all the above remain in default. Both China and the old Soviet Union have settled their differences with British bondholders at least (see pages 44 and 64). Certain countries, particularly those of South America have, over recent years, almost wholly cleared their debts as has Bulgaria. An outstanding default restricts a country or company from issuing new paper on certain international markets which provides some incentive to clear past debts.

Although Confederate bonds remain unpaid their stock market quote has been dropped, but this did not happen until the 1890s. The State of Mississippi has been the subject of numerous legal actions, but so far, to no avail. The story is told on pages 86-88.

THE DIFFERENCE BETWEEN BONDS & SHARES

Before adding some technical background it might be appropriate to identify a potentially confusing language quirk. "Shares" are more usually known as "stocks" in the United States, whereas "stocks" can mean bonds in England (simple really!) To make it easy here bonds will always be bonds and "stocks and shares" will be described as stocks or shares at random!

Collecting bonds and shares necessarily requires a basic knowledge of finance, but the depth of that knowledge is very much up to the individual scripophilist. As a minimum, this is all you need to know: apart from trading profits, a company of whatever size, obtains its finances from two main sources, namely shareholders (the owners of the company) and lenders. The latter may be banks, governments or private individuals, who usually provide funds for a limited period at an agreed rate of interest. If things go badly for the company, the lenders still get paid (unless they go *really* badly), but the shareholders may well not as they have no guaranteed return on their investment. Conversely, of course, when the company is successful and business is booming the shareholders stand to benefit most as they have taken the greater risk and will reap the larger returns accordingly. Loans to a company take several forms, the most common of which is the bank overdraft, another is through the issue of bonds.

As a general simplification, share certificates are evidence of an individual's investment in the ownership of a company, and bonds are evidence of debt.

THE ORIGINS & DEVELOPMENT OF BOND & SHARE TRADING

The earliest known trading of both bonds and shares may be traced back to the merchants of ancient Mesopotamia, around 2000 BC. The first "shares" are believed to have been "Temple Days" which were issued in the form of clay tablets and represented an individual's purchase of an annual day of the Temple. The share entitled the owner to all the income arising on that particular day and the share itself could be sold or broken down into fractional periods. A similar system is thought to have existed in Egypt some time later but it was not until AD 954 that varied and active share trading truly began. The location was Amalfi in Southern Italy and the evidence lies in the earliest known written commercial code of the Italian maritime republics — "La Tabula de Amalpha". The code permitted the sale of shares in maritime trading ventures and sales by shareholders to others.

From AD 1100 bond trading became active in the Italian city states of Genoa, Venice, Amalfi and Florence. The bonds which were mainly issued to finance those states were known as "Monti", a format which continued throughout the eighteenth century. Later similar bonds issued with the involvement of the church are known as Monti di Pieta and these date from the mid fifteenth century (Perugia was the earliest dated 1462). Such items are difficult but not impossible to acquire and are sought after by many collectors.

From 1530, Antwerp became the financial centre for the merchants of Europe. Its ruler, the Duke of Brabant (who also happened to be King of Spain) built a new bourse and encouraged trading in all kinds of financial instruments through low taxes and minimal regulation. Bonds issued by the Court of the Netherlands, the English Crown and the City of London amongst others were actively traded in Antwerp which soon became the source of funds for the Kings of Europe.

Antwerp's reign as Financial Capital ended in 1566 with the outbreak of civil war and its place was quickly taken by Amsterdam which dominated share trading in joint stock companies throughout the seventeenth century. The Amsterdam Stock Exchange was formed in 1611 but most of its business was concentrated in the shares of the Dutch East India Company (founded 1602) and the Dutch West India Company (1621).

London

Following Antwerp's demise Sir Thomas Gresham, who had been Britain's "Crown Agent" in that city resolved to create a major financial centre in London and on his return, built the Royal Exchange with that object in mind after raising funds from the 20 senior Livery Companies. The building was completed in 1567 but burnt down in the Great Fire of 1666. The creation of many joint stock companies, including the formation of the Bank of England (in 1694) and the East India Company (in 1600) ensured an active share market and one which proved to be so speculative, controversial and disruptive to other financial activities taking place in the Royal Exchange that the share brokers were expelled from the building in 1696 and forced to continue their dealings in the coffee shops of Exchange Alley ("Jonathans" in particular). It was not until 1773 that a group of brokers acquired a building of their own in Threadneadle Street and so established the London Stock Exchange.

The scandal surrounding the South Sea Company with its eventual collapse in 1720 and the later financial crashes, particularly that of 1825, did little to foster a permanent feeling of confidence. However, such events did finally contribute to a more regulated and progressive market for share trading.

Early American Activity

Share trading in America prior to the Revolution was very limited and largely controlled by the British. Activity in the financial markets really only began with the issue of bonds to finance the Revolutionary troops in the 1770s. Although the New York Stock Exchange was founded in 1792, even by 1820 only 30 different securities were traded there. Immediately following the Revolution, Philadelphia was the country's financial centre but by 1790, New York had taken over. During the nineteenth century approximately 250 different stock exchanges were opened (and mostly, closed) across the country.

REGISTERED v BEARER

Many early certificates, whether shares, bonds or other loan documents, were issued 'To Bearer'. This meant that the investment in the company could be sold or passed on to a new individual without reference to the company concerned. Physical possession of the document — assuming it wasn't stolen or obtained by fraudulent means — was all important. This system kept records to a minimum and put the onus of dividend or interest distribution on the investor rather than the company, which of course was unaware of the names and addresses of its financiers. So far as investors were concerned a notable benefit was secrecy; no one, not even the tax-collector, could ascertain a person's investment from a company's records.

This emphasis on bearer shares continued for many years and in some countries, such as

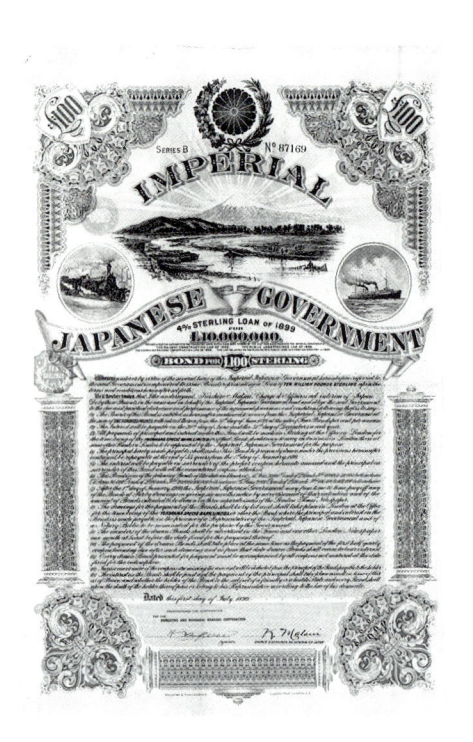

Japan has repaid all its bonds but occasionally one such as this appears on the collectors market. It is both rare and attractive.

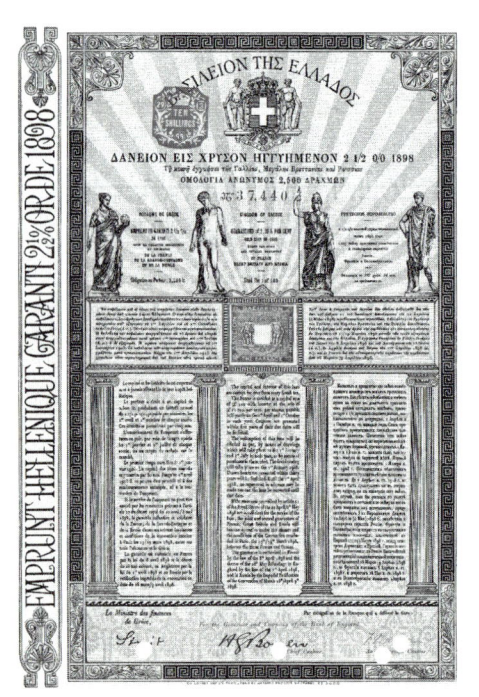

Kingdom of Greece 1898 Gold Loan. The whole of this loan was held by the Bank of England for many years.

Switzerland, is still the norm. Many governments, however, felt the need to tighten up on controls and imposed a requirement for share registration — to the benefit of company registrars!

By now, you will probably have realized the significance of registered versus bearer to the collector. As a bearer share is not issued to anyone in particular it does not have to be cancelled and re-issued when traded, thus the number of bearer shares is limited to the issued capital of the company, an amount usually printed on the certificates. On the other hand, a registered share must be re-registered whenever sold, and the original cancelled or destroyed. As there is no limit to the number of times a share may change hands, there is similarly no limit to the number of certificates which may ultimately exist.

So far as bonds are concerned, most are 'bearer'. They are usually issued by a company or State and may be held by anyone, anywhere in the world (exchange controls permitting). Considerable detail is printed on the document itself giving the investor exact instructions for obtaining interest and eventual repayment of principal. Occasionally, as with the Chinese for example, instructions are printed in several languages. During their life they change hands frequently, and if lost a duplicate may be issued, but clearly identified as such. Thus the number of bonds issued by a particular borrower is known exactly, and because such information is of interest to the investor, it is almost always printed on the bond itself.

REPAYMENT

The terms 'issued', 'redeemed' and 'outstanding' require some explanation. Reference has already been made to the relatively unchanged mechanics governing the issue and repayment of bonds over the years. Bonds were not only issued in the past to build the early railroads of the Americas or finance Imperial China's balance of payments, they continue to be issued today by governments and companies in even greater numbers — albeit not so decoratively. Their beginning and end is summarized as follows:

> Detailed information on the borrower is prepared and a group of underwriters (usually banks) is assembled. A few of this group are selected as the issuing banks. The bond is then launched into the market.
>
> Bonds are a debt, and as such must be repaid over a

The less interesting the subject, the more decorative can be the certificate! This superbly engraved £20 debenture from 1913 of the Genoa District Waterworks depicts the port of Genoa with the Columbus Monument clearly visible.

specified number of years, not simply at the end of the borrowing term. This is an important feature and you will understand the process better by studying the small print on a particular bond. All state the period of the loan and also indicate from which year repayment begins, so that by the end of the total period all bonds have been fully redeemed. Thus, after the grace period, there will always be some bonds which are outstanding and some which have been repaid. As time passes, the outstanding bonds diminish in number.

It is the calculation of the number of bonds redeemed which can cause most problems for the scripophilist seeking to ascertain rarity.

There are two alternative methods adopted by borrowers for redemption of bonds. The simplest (albeit least common) is that chosen by the Chinese. In this case a constant percentage of bonds was repaid each year; thus, if the loan was for a period of fifty years and twenty-five years elapsed before default, then it is correct to assume that fifty per cent of the original bonds should have been repaid.

The more usual procedure, however, complicates the calculation. In this case, the total monetary value of the loan including interest is divided by the number of repaying years. The resulting figure represents the amount of money which the borrower must put aside annually in order to meet interest payments and the gradual redemption of the bonds (known as the 'sinking fund'). Unfortunately, this is not as simple as it sounds, for in early years most of the sinking fund goes towards interest and very few bonds are redeemed (similar to a real estate mortgage); as time passes, however, an increasing amount of the principal is repaid but it is a complex calculation to work out the exact number of redemptions at a specific time.

In view of the many potential pitfalls in attempting to accurately determine the number of outstanding bonds of a particular issue, collectors should seek out the detailed stock market records.

One final point on redemption relates to the choice of which bonds are selected for payment. This is often determined by lot and the serial numbers of those bonds to be redeemed are published in the press. Such bonds may be described as "drawn" and this hand written word often appears on those drawn for repayment.

DEBENTURES & OTHER FINANCIAL INSTRUMENTS

Apart from bonds and shares the scripophilist may come across other financial documents, which may be summarised as follows:
- Debentures. Similar in form and function to bonds and always of a limited issue to cover a specific borrowing need. The debenture, for tax reasons, proved most popular with British companies.
- Scrip Certificates. Usually these represent fractions of bonds issued either in advance of the bonds themselves, possibly on receipt of a part payment, or to make up a particular investment sum. They are rarely attractive.
- Share Warrants. Usually bearer these are similar to shares in appearance but often provided the investor with a fixed interest income and the option to convert to equity at a later date.
- Transfer Certificates. Whenever a registered share was sold a transfer certificate had to be completed identifying seller and buyer. Some early transfer certificates can look as good as the shares themselves and it is easy to confuse the two.

This share in the Russian Tobacco Company, issued in 1915, is a superb example of Waterlow engraving.

PRINTING AND ENGRAVING

Some time has already been spent explaining the difference between 'bearer' and 'registered' certificates, from which the reader will appreciate the dangers of forgery in the case of the former. It was primarily for this reason that companies or governments issuing bearer stock went to great lengths and expense to deter the prospective forger.

TECHNIQUES

As with banknotes, the most effective deterrent was a combination of high quality paper, skilled engraving and intricate design. The same companies which printed banknotes and postage stamps were employed as producers of bonds and share certificates. Early engraving techniques involved cutting into a copper or steel plate with the use of tools such as a burin or graver. Skilled engravers knew how deep to cut the plate in order to create different depths of design and perspective. Up to the early nineteenth century copper plates were used which, being softer than the steel plates commonly employed thereafter, had a limited life.

Share certificates of the Ethiopian Railway are dominated by the superb vignette with the text almost appearing as an afterthought.

The four names appearing most frequently as printers of certificates are Waterlow & Sons, Bradbury Wilkinson and De La Rue of England and the American Bank Note Company of the United States. From 1858, the latter incorporated seven other American printing companies and in 1879 took Bradbury Wilkinson under its wing, followed by the Canadian Bank Note Company in 1911.

The security printing department of each firm held a number of engravers trained for specific tasks. Highest status was afforded the engraver of portraits, as this entailed the greatest amount of skill and experience. There would be another who specialized in vignette, such as landscapes, buildings, trains and groups of people, and a third who was the letter engraver entrusted with transmitting the name of the company or country, text, and other details.

Some time in the early nineteenth century the American, Jacob Perkins (who later settled in England and formed Perkins Bacon, Crown Agents) invented the transference method of security printing. This allowed for relatively fast production of large numbers of certificates while still maintaining the individuality necessary to prevent easy forgery. Each engraver worked on a separate plate, using up only the area allotted for his specialized task. The engravings on each plate were then transferred to a master plate.

Colours were applied by means of separate plates or by use of the lithographic method whereby a 'stone' is waxed and the areas which will later take the ink are scraped away. Another mechanical process was instrumental in the engraving techniques found on bonds and shares from about the

By 1919 the Chilean Northern had become part of the Antofagasta & Bolivia Railway Company. These fine looking debentures were engraved by Bradbury Wilkinson who used the same train vignette on bonds of the Manila Railway Company.

The shares of Lloyd Bank (Hungary) are some of the most elaborate seen.

mid-nineteenth century and helped to make forgery difficult, if not impossible. Asa Spencer, a founder of the American Bank Note Company, invented the geometrical lathe for making ornamental borders. By means of discs and gear wheels which moved together, a series of complex patterns were formed by a diamond-tipped point moving over a plate. An infinite variety of settings — and hence patterns — was possible.

DESIGN

Companies or countries normally suggested their own designs, which is why Chinese and Russian bonds and shares look distinctly Chinese or Russian despite the fact that some of the Russian and probably all of the Chinese were designed and printed by western firms. The art departments of security printing firms produced designs for the approval of the client — as well as lettering, these often contained vignettes related to the country, town or organization issuing the certificates. After approval of the design, the artist composed a detailed watercolour to be copied by engravers. Certificates engraved by American printing firms, in particular from the nineteenth century onwards, are characterized by the liberal use of cherubs and pseudo-Grecian mythological figures intermingling with trains and other signs of modern industry.

Fine example of a "Specimen" bond for the Royal Siamese Government 1936 loan.

It is often interesting to compare designs and a self-trained eye can soon begin to spot common features. These features may be the result of a government, such as Russia, wanting to preserve an image of consistency or, as is more usual, a printer using existing designs in different permutations. For example, many of the trains appearing on US railroad certificates reappear on both Chinese and Russian banknotes.

The use of existing part plates naturally reduced the cost of printing but another alternative was also employed for the production of registered share certificates. Not being bearer (and thus less open to forgery), these could be 'neatly lithographed or printed letterpress, without incurring the cost of engraving a specially designed plate . . .' as advertised by Waterlow in their General Catalogue of 1912.

However, not all bearer material was as carefully prepared as suggested here. There are cases, and the bonds issued by the US Confederacy are prime examples, where scant attention was paid to the dangers of forgery. Out of the 170 or so different Confederate bond types, only four were engraved. Those four are the Tri-value Cotton Bonds of 1863, which were clearly produced in Europe but it is not known by whom. Other Confederate bonds were printed on poor quality paper, which accounts for their often poor condition today. Ten different printing houses were used to produce the certificates in Charleston, Columbia, Richmond and New Orleans.

Gold is not always beautiful! Despite the original printers confirming that they had never produced a Rolls-Royce share certificate complete with gold car, the auctioneers who sold this item refused to believe it was not genuine. No doubt, as a limited piece of forgery it will appreciate in value faster than the real thing!

SPECIMENS

No certificates are accepted unseen from a printer. No matter how much checking has been done, there is always the chance of a typographical error creeping in and causing untold financial damage to the issuer. For this reason, prior to final printing a small quantity of "specimen" certificates will be produced by the printer for final verification. These items will (usually) be clearly marked "specimens" either by means of overprint or perforated cancellation holes. In some cases they can be further identified by a "0000" serial number.

In recent years, the collecting of specimens, has increased in popularity. They have the advantages of usually being in mint condition and also rarer than the end product. On the other hand they lack signatures, company seals, revenue stamps and lots of dirty thumb prints, all of which contribute to the appeal of the "genuine" share!

FUTURE DEVELOPMENTS

Despite the engravers' efforts there have been occasions, especially in recent years, when the temptation to forge has been too great. Most such forgery concentrates on the live aspects of bonds and shares and because of this (and the sheer physical effort of handling large quantities of paper) stock exchanges across the world have been exploring ways of eliminating the documents themselves and facilitating share and bond transfers through computer databases. Such actions will inevitably increase interest in early material.

As the hobby gains momentum forgeries designed to fool collectors may increase. So far there have been relatively few cases and most "reproductions" are easy to spot and rarely sold in the first instance as originals. Collectors are, however, advised to watch out for the obviously wrong, such as un-watermarked modern paper, lack of embossed company seal, or, even worse, signatures made in biro or felt tipped pen on certificates from the last century!

A recent example of deception concerns shares of Rolls-Royce Ltd., a particularly plain certificate on which some thoughtful entrepreneur added a gold Rolls-Royce!

ART FOR MONEY'S SAKE

Those more interested in the work of Renoir or Rembrandt may find the relatively simple graphic art employed in scrip design somewhat lacking in depth. But is it? Commercial art has different objectives and in the case of bonds and shares, that objective was simply to persuade potential investors to part with their money and discourage forgery.

The novelty of industry was portrayed on many early certificates with views of multi-chimneyed factories vigorously polluting the atmosphere for the good of mankind. Such evidence of manufacture was reassuring to prospective shareholders and, for many, a picture of the establishment on a share certificate was the nearest they actually came to "seeing" their investments. Thus, factories, railway bridges and mine workings were favourite decorations on early share certificates. For certain companies, these signs of property and activity went no further than the certificates themselves, and on more than one occasion investors were encouraged to part with their money through fanciful views of company activity.

It was, of course, inevitable that the contemporary artistic style was reflected in the design of certificates of that period. For some countries contemporary art was of paramount importance, others took a more pragmatic view. British certificates, for example, have been consistently plain with few frills. US railroad bonds have concentrated on locomotive vignettes, whilst others, particularly French certificates of the 1920s, are of clear 'art nouveau' derivation and display a marked preference for scantily clad maidens irrespective of the true company activity. Some shares, were actually designed by well known artists, such as those of "Paris France" by Alphonse Mucha. Indeed most French material is extremely ornate, as are also many of the Spanish and Italian shares.

Art Nouveau was superseded by Art Deco in the late 1920s and certificates of this period and style are keenly collected, often commanding high prices. Many examples can be found amongst French, Spanish and German shares.

But art takes many forms, and precise design work can be as pleasing as the most elaborate images — both have the advantage of making the forger's task that much more difficult. The portrayal of a naked lady on a recent Playboy Enterprises share certificate can hardly be considered a cultural contribution, but it nevertheless displays the company's 'product' as succinctly as a smoking chimney describes an active factory (see page 26).

Hispano Suiza is perhaps best known for its high quality cars well favoured by European royal families, but the share certificates, of which there were several issues, are classic examples of art in scripophily. Designed by the Spanish commercial artist Ramon Casa i Carbo, the share depicts the Italian actress, Teresa Mariani next to her Hispano Suiza.

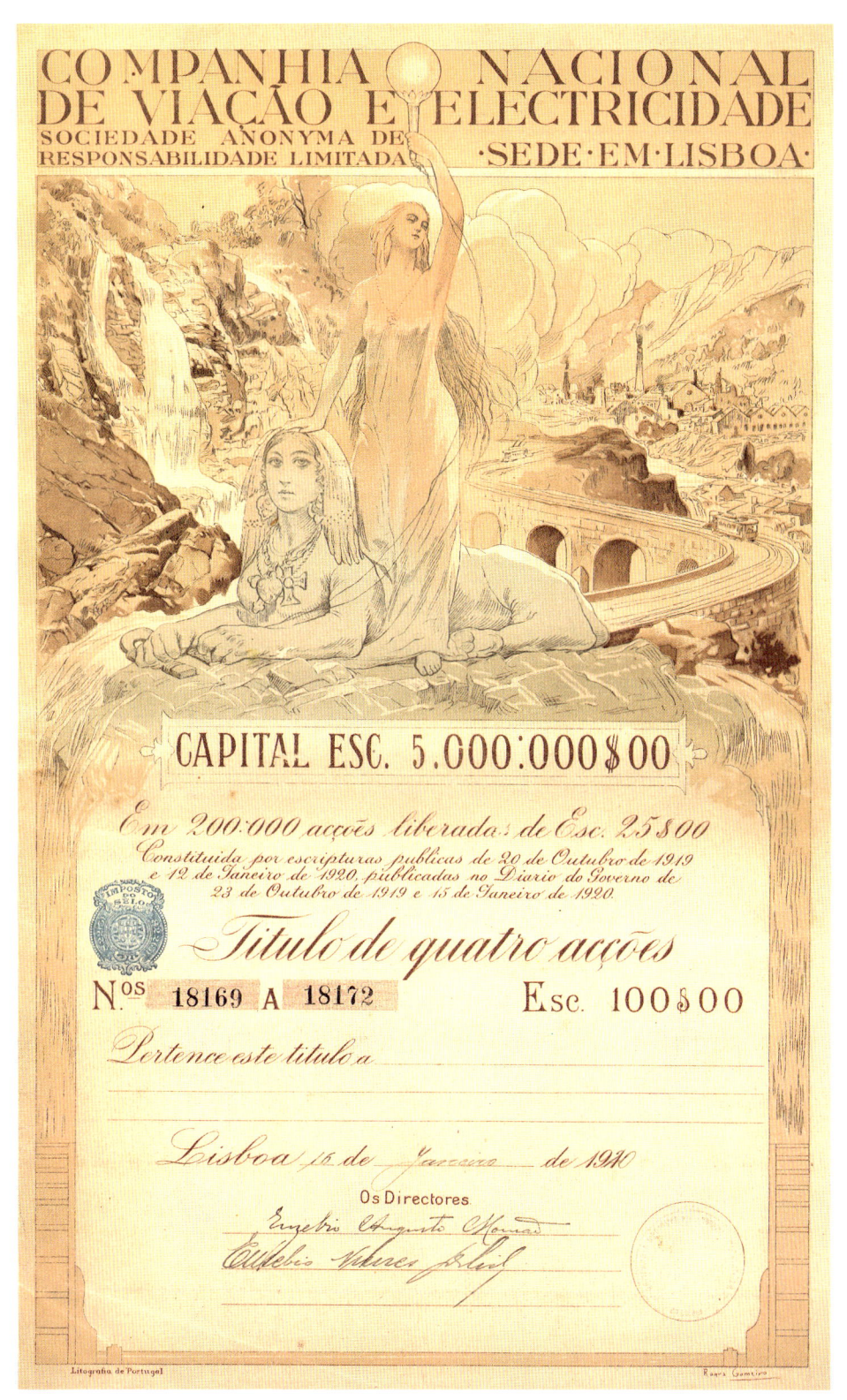

Portuguese shares of the 1920s were often elaborate and of art deco style. This share in the Companhia Nacional de Viacao e Electricidade is no exception.

Current stock certificates of Playboy are rather more modest than this "traditional" version from the 1980s, replete with the facsimile signature of Hugh Hefner.

SHARES OF HISTORY

History and art are as much a part of scripophily as economics. Just as finance has played its part in history since the beginnings of trade, so scripophily gives us the opportunity to view that involvement through the financial documents themselves.

There are perhaps (and no doubt someone will disagree) 5 clearly defined periods of world economic development:
1. Early and primitive commodity trading.
2. The establishment of the Trading Companies in the 16th and 17th centuries.
3. The Industrial Revolution of the 1780s.
4. Railway construction from the 1830s.
5. The marketing and technology age of the 20th century.

So far, scripophily has not embraced the first period, largely due to lack of research and readily available material. It does however come into its own with the early trading companies of Holland, Britain and Spain. Certificates from these companies are both rare and expensive and apart from those from Spain, rather plain in appearance.

Most of the material collected today post-dates the Industrial Revolution which may be regarded as the starting point for the formation of so many major industries now taken for granted. Many of these industries were of such a size (iron and steel, canals, railways, etc.) that they could only be financed

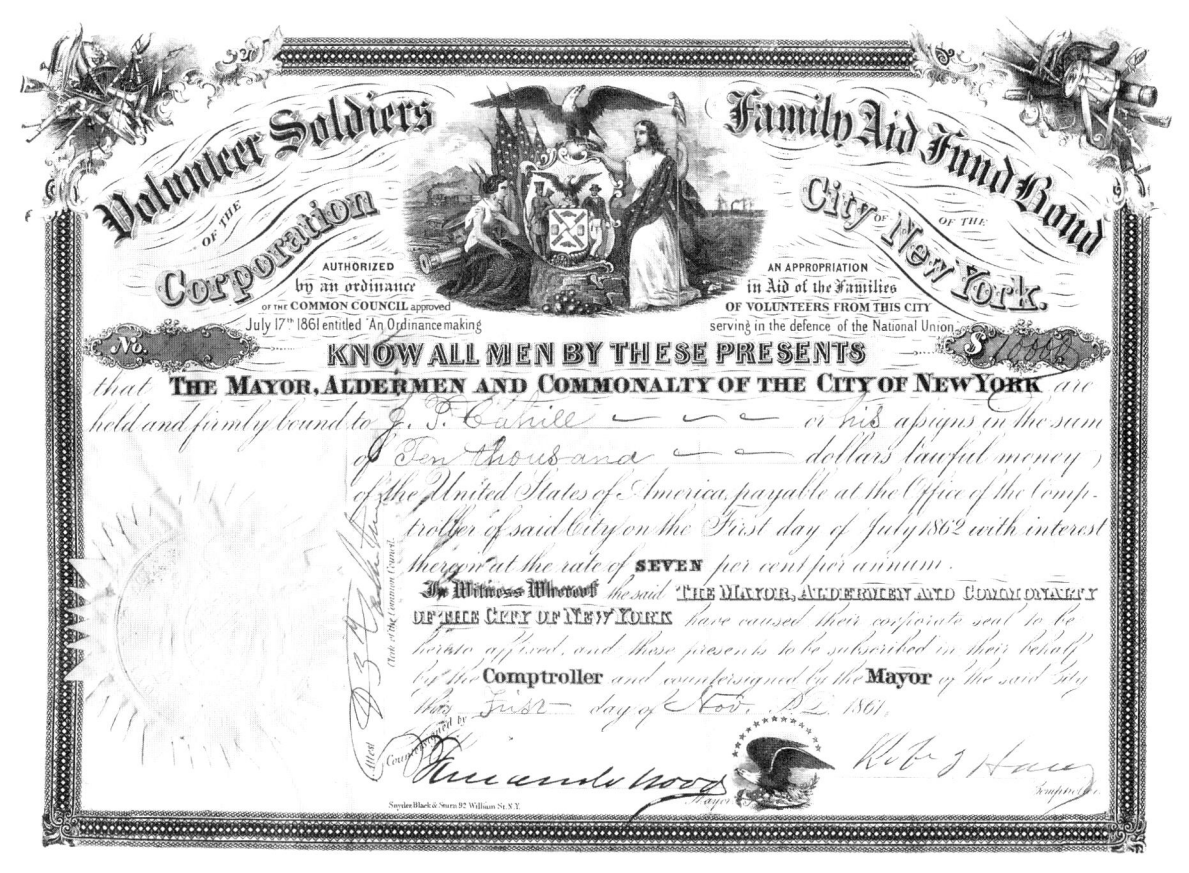

Not all bonds from the American Civil War were issued by the Confederacy. The purpose of this one was to raise money to pay to the families of the volunteers.

by the joint efforts of many investors rather than the lone entrepreneur. The establishment of an increasing number of companies resulted in the creation of share certificates of all kinds and their survival today provides the basis of scripophily.

Whereas most collectable material originated as a result of the formation of commercial enterprises, some had other objectives such as the funding of the Red Cross, the American Revolutionary Army, the American Civil War and even the beginnings of Israel. Some are a reminder of countries whose independence is no more.

THE STAR OF TEXAS

Following the eventual defeat of the Spaniards in Texas in 1836, a republic was founded led by Stephen F. Austin. The Texans' original objective was to join the United States, but it was not until 1845 that this was achieved, during which time the State operated as an independent country. Nowhere is this more clearly highlighted than in the bonds issued to finance its development. Many were signed by Austin and bear the famous 'Lone Star' symbol. Several issues were denominated in £ sterling as well as US $, indicating the close economic links with Britain which were encouraged by the State as a means of applying political pressure on the United States.

THE AMERICAN CIVIL WAR

The first shot was fired on 12 April 1861, when Southern troops under the command of General P. G. T. Beauregard, one of the most flamboyant characters of the war and whose picture featured on two Confederate bond issues, launched their 40-hour bombardment of Fort Sumter, Charleston. But it was not until 21 July that the two armies met at Bull Run for the first major engagement.

Bull Run was a disaster for the North and their performance over the next two years was little improved. Major reasons were lack of military leadership and an unfounded overconfidence at the outset. Both sides felt the war would be short-lived and neither called up troops in sufficient numbers. The North frequently enrolled men for 90 day stints, and pay was invariably late. Some Northern (Union) bond issues were used to provide financial incentives to volunteers, for example, the State of New York 7% loan, "Payment of Bounties to Volunteers". But despite the ingenuity and military skill of the Confederate General, Robert E. Lee, the North's superior resources of men and materiel eventually triumphed on 9 April 1865 when Lee was surrounded and forced to surrender by General Ulysses S. Grant at Appomatox Court House. Within one month the war was ended.

The lack of financial independence of the Confederacy resulted in the need to raise large foreign loans. The endless demand for cotton, in Britain and France in particular, made the raising of such loans feasible as many were guaranteed against cotton bales. Some, such as the 1863 loan of £3 million, were even denominated in cotton effectively incorporating a futures contract. Some £800,000 of these bonds were redeemed against cotton during the war, and subsequently destroyed, but when the Confederacy collapsed in 1865 the bales set aside as security for the balance were seized, sold or burnt by the victors. The amount of money borrowed and eventually defaulted by the Confederate States was enormous, with one issue alone exceeding $147 million.

The history of the occasion is further emphasized by the portraits displayed on the bonds themselves. Most Confederate leaders are depicted on one or more issues. As well as such notables as General 'Stonewall' Jackson and President Jefferson Davis, the whole political cabinet got coverage (bond numbers refer to the Criswell catalogue; see bibliography).

NAME	POSITION	BONDS ON WHICH THEY APPEAR
Jefferson Davis	President	4, 85, 86, 95, 125
Alexander Stephens	Vice-President	70, 123
Robert Toombs (Georgia)	Secretary of State	37
Christopher Memminger (S. Carolina)	Secretary of the Treasury	59, 84, 87, 88, 92, 97, 98, 102, 110, 111, 124
L. P. Walker (Alabama)	Secretary of War	21
Stephen R. Mallory (Florida)	Secretary of the Navy	33, 34, 40, 663, 67, 89
John H. Regan (Texas)	Postmaster General	36, 62, 101
J. P. Benjamin (Louisiana)	Attorney General	31, 43, 57, 60, 61, 65, 71, 75, 100

Later cabinet reshuffles resulted in J. P. Benjamin becoming Secretary of State and George W. Randolph Secretary of War (bonds 422, 64, 68). Not only were Confederate celebrities portrayed, but also the famous founders of America. George Washington figured prominently on many issues, and even Benjamin Franklin and John C. Calhoun made their appearance — the objective being to convince foreign investors of the legality of their cause.

Despite being issued well after the first "gold rush" this Arizona registered share says it all in title and colour.

Shares in the Jewish Colonial Trust are well sought after. Their intrinsic history and vignettes depicting trade, industry, agriculture and religion (the "wailing wall" now known as the "Western Wall") add considerably to value.

PALESTINE AND ISRAEL

On the other side of the Atlantic and over thirty years later, another cause began to surface and was reflected by an interesting share issue.

The Jewish Colonial Trust formed in 1899 represented the aspirations of the Zionist movement led by Dr Theodor Herzl towards establishment of a Jewish state. It was intended to be the financial arm — a sort of Jewish East India company — to gather money for building industries, railways and the buying of land in Palestine. The Jewish Colonial Trust, chartered in London, arose out of the first and second Zionist Congresses in Basel which decided to create an independent financial institution '. . . to develop colonization, the natural resources, industries of the country and to create working opportunities'.

By 1956 there were over 100,000 shareholders; however, the institution seems to have been more enthusiastically received among the poor than the rich and this may be one reason for its failure to achieve its original aims. Even an early supporter of the Trust, a Dr Gaster admitted that they were merely building the first rung of the ladder. Did anyone imagine that the whole of Palestine could be bought for £2 million he asked rhetorically? 'Not for £100 million could one buy that land.' He said that he would welcome the rich and that they were wrong to work against the Trust. It had been called a trust, he said, because the money of the Jewish nations in Europe would be kept in trust for the Jewish nation in Palestine.

The Trust may not have been the main instrument in the formation of the Jewish State as it wished, but it did at least have one major achievement. It led to the creation of a Jewish bank, its present-day successor being Bank Leumi.

Denominated in £ sterling, confederate dollars and cotton, these finely engraved Confederate Cotton bonds issued by Erlanger and Schroder use a commodity hedge (guaranteeing the price of cotton at a future date). 4 denominations were issued in 1863, £100, £200, £500 and £1000.

PART 2

Collecting Themes

INTRODUCTION

Deciding on a collecting theme is the first and most important step in starting a collection, consequently this section takes up a disproportionate share of the book. Several themes are looked at in varying detail not with the intention of offering a comprehensive analysis of the subject but to provide you, as a collector, with a taste for the certificates available and some of the history behind them.

Choosing a collecting theme at the outset is a difficult, albeit enjoyable, task. Some may wish to defer the decision by first purchasing a selection of material, such as the 'starter packs' provided by some dealers, this approach is fine and gives the collector a personal feel of the alternatives; others may prefer to go directly to their chosen field. Whichever approach is chosen, it is important to settle on a theme and concentrate on collecting rather than simply accumulating.

The section has been divided into two, the first by country and the second by subject. Such a division implies a degree of exclusivity which is unfortunate as both subjects and countries inevitably overlap. Those who collect "railways", for example, will inevitably cross national frontiers, whilst those who choose to collect material from one country will, of course, also become specialists in mines, banks and other industrial ventures within their chosen domain. Where possible repetition has been avoided but as some readers may only wish to look at certain sections, some repetition is inevitable.

AUSTRALIA

Being a relatively "young" country with a small population, Australia may be thought to have little to offer the scripophilist. This is certainly not the case. The country, because of its size, distance from the West and huge mineral resources, makes an ideal collecting theme with material mirroring its economic and social development.

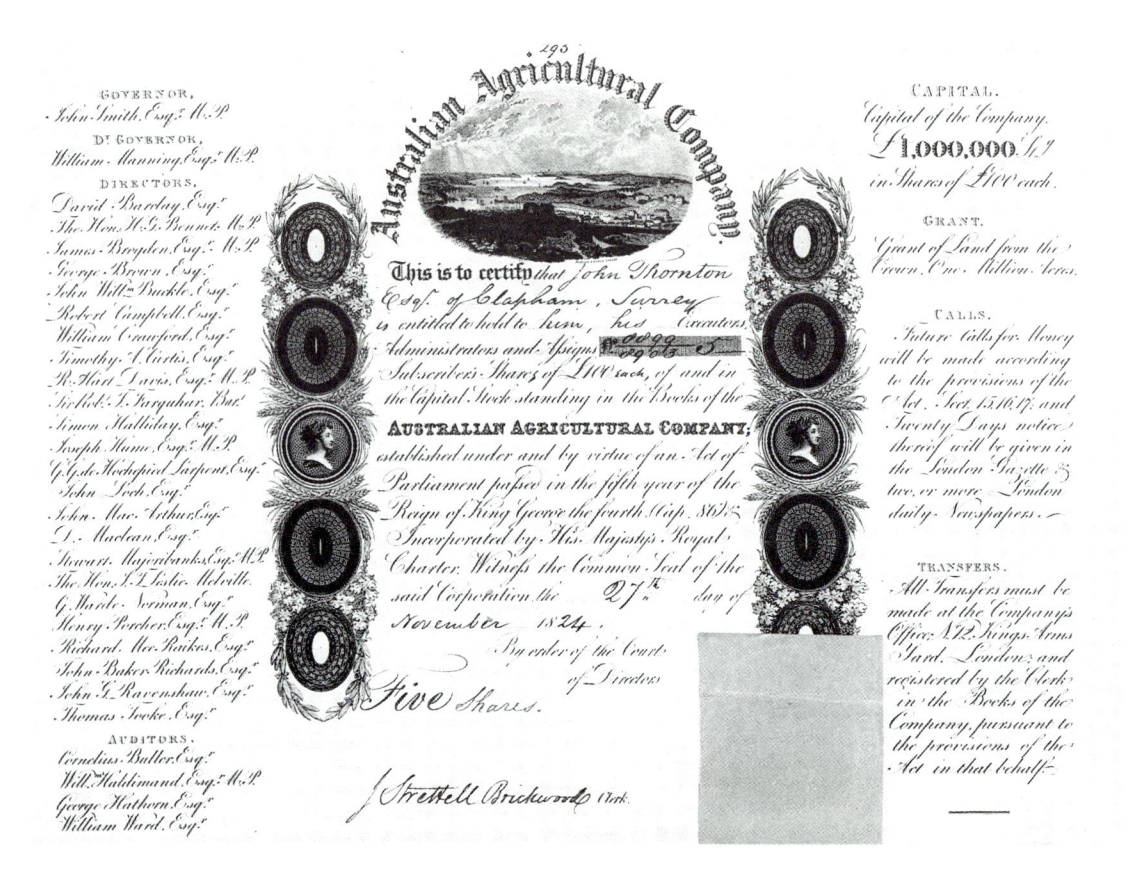

The Australian Agricultural Company shares are some of the earliest and finest known from Australia. The centre vignette is of Sydney.

EARLY HISTORY

Twenty-seven years elapsed after the settlement landing, at Sydney Cove in 1788, before the first out-of-town road was constructed. In 1802 the population was no more than 6,000 persons and 8,632 sheep, but it was the latter which were primarily responsible for the country's early growth.

Until this period most of the high-quality wool needed for Britain's mills had come from Saxony. For strategic reasons the country wished to reduce this dependence on Europe and the opportunity to source large amounts of top-quality wool from Australia fitted the bill perfectly. The Australian Agricultural Company was formed in 1824 to primarily produce Merino wool (from imported Saxony sheep) for sale to England. The company's founders included eight directors of the Bank of England and several from the English East India Company. Shareholders had the option of eventually taking their profits or converting shares into land grants; many chose the latter. Share certificates of the Company are occasionally seen today and are some of the most elaborate in scripophily.

The early years to 1850 were centred around the pastoral development of the country and as farming expanded so the major towns were founded: Brisbane in 1824, Perth in 1829, Adelaide in 1836 and Melbourne in 1835. Banks were formed, with the earliest being the Bank of New South Wales (1817), the largest shareholder of which (Samuel Terry) was an ex-convict deported from Britain for stealing socks in 1800 and later known as the "Rothschild of Botany Bay"! The first known "Bank of Australia" was formed in 1833 but collapsed ten years later during the banking crisis of the time. Certificates in both these banks are known but like the Agricultural company, are likely to be expensive. All three are printed on vellum. However, it was 1851 before the real fireworks started.

Lady Loch Gold Mines. Typical West Australian mining share registered in London.

GOLD AND MINERALS

Mention is made later of the great gold rushes of the mid nineteenth century. Many of those early prospectors who had made their fortune in California moved on to Australia. One such, Edward Hargreaves discovered gold at Bathurst, New South Wales, in 1851. The effect was dramatic, generating an upsurge in immigrants from across the world and the formation of numerous spin-off companies. The first mining company — imaginatively entitled "The Australian Mining Company" was formed as early as 1845 and from that time on, numerous companies were formed and their shares traded on a myriad of local stock exchanges scattered across the gold fields. Gold was not the only mineral; tin, silver and precious stones were also found and by 1879 steam drawn railways were starting to appear, two of the first being the "St Kilda & Brighton Railway Company" (1857) and the "Melbourne Suburban Railway Company" (1859).

The second great gold rush occurred in the West with the discovery of rich seams east of Perth at Southern Cross. These were followed by the major fields of Coolgardie (1892) and Kalgoorlie (1893). Many famous names appear on early mining shares, such as: Herbert Hoover who came to Australia

By the time he was 30, Whitaker Wright had made and lost two fortunes and had been Chairman of the Philadelphia Mining Exchange. His companies, of which London & Globe was the most famous, were manipulated to maximum effect and in 1904 Wright was tried and convicted on 26 counts of fraud. Within 30 minutes of hearing the sentence he swallowed cyanide. The London & Globe financed construction of London's Baker Street and Waterloo Underground.

as a mining engineer and was active in several mines notably "Sons of Gwalia"; Claude de Bernales, one of the most successful and notorious promoters of the time; and Whittaker Wright, an English speculator eventually jailed for fraud.

Mineral discoveries continued (and indeed still continue) throughout the latter part of the century and in 1883 Charles Rasp first discovered the varied riches of Broken Hill resulting in the formation of the country's largest private enterprise, "Broken Hill Proprietary Company" (BHP). However, it was the growth of secondary industries which caused a marked shift in population from the country to the towns, eventually making Sydney and Melbourne two of the world's largest cities. The formation and development of the more formal Stock Exchanges (Melbourne 1860, Sydney 1871 and Perth 1896) gradually put an end to the notorious methods of share trading such as the "open call" system where shares were simply auctioned to the highest bidder.

CERTIFICATES AND COLLECTORS

It is not easy to build a really sizeable collection of Australian material. Early shares such as those described are both costly and rare, whilst later ones, although more plentiful, do not exist in the large numbers one would expect. This should not be a reason to avoid the theme, a challenge can prove most satisfying and a collection embracing contemporary photographs, company prospectuses and other related ephemera should prove an exciting target.

CANADA

With the break up of the Soviet Union, Canada is now the largest country in the world, albeit one of the most sparsely populated. So far as the scripophilist is concerned, the country offers a wide choice of material ranging from gold mines to railways.

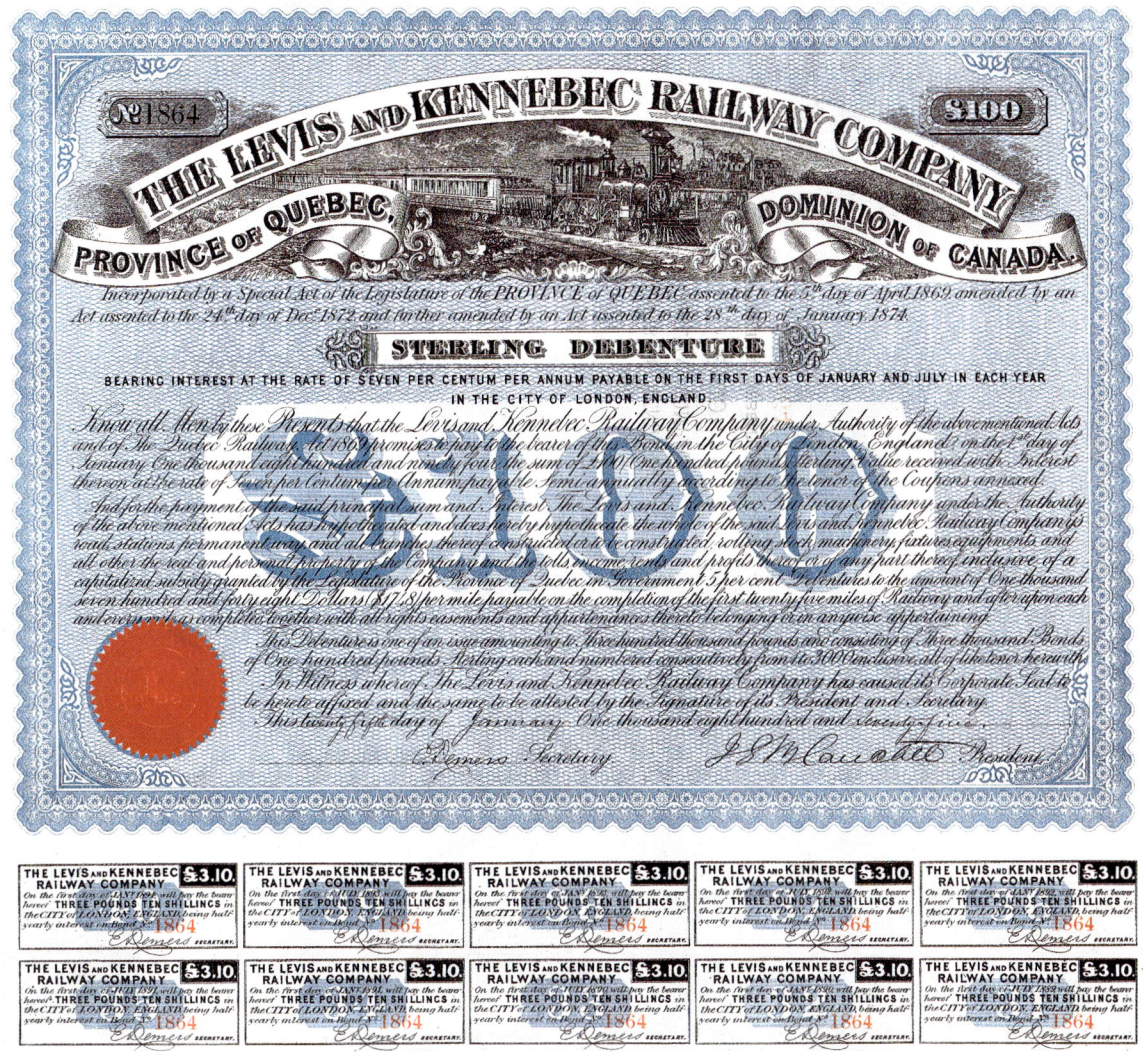

Initially running from Levis to Scott, the Levis & Kennebec Railway was opened in 1875 and was eventually purchased by the Quebec Central at a Sheriff's sale.

    Apart from the activities of the early fur traders and the Hudson's Bay Company in particular, not a great deal happened on the industrial front until the formation of the "Dominion" in 1869 and the purchase by the Government of Rupert Land from the Hudson's Bay Company for £300,000. The need to strengthen links in the newly created country led to the need for greater railway development and this was spearheaded by the incorporation of the Canadian Pacific in 1881, backed by Barings and which, on completion connected Montreal to Vancouver. Several railways existed prior to this date with one of the earliest being the Great Western Railroad financed by the issue of debentures by Oxford County in 1850. That line proved to be a financial success which is more than can be said of the much larger Grand Trunk Railway which was opened in 1856 and once again largely financed by Barings — to their cost! The line eventually collapsed in 1919 and became a part of the Government owned Canadian National Railways.

MINING

Canada is one of the richest countries in the world for minerals but difficult terrain and climate meant that development has been relatively recent. The most celebrated beginning is possibly the Klondike Gold Rush of 1898, an event made famous by Charlie Chaplin. The discovery of gold in Klondike Creek came at the end of a worldwide depression and led to the inevitable influx of hopefuls from the United States, Europe and Russia. Over the next years, numerous finds were made covering the whole range of minerals, one of the major ones being silver at Cobalt in 1930. Canada is now the largest producer of nickel and zinc in the world and a major source of asbestos, oil, gas, copper and gold. Share certificates in companies specialising in these areas are reasonably easy to obtain but not as easy as one would expect. It would appear that the Canadian Registrars were rather more careful in looking after cancelled stock than their southern neighbours.

San Antonio Land & Irrigation Company. Speculative land development company. The share bears the facsimile signature of F. S. Pearson, a colleague of Alfred Lowenstein. Pearson perished in the Lusitania in 1915

ALFRED LOWENSTEIN ET AL

Two of Canada's most well known entrepreneurs whose signatures are not difficult to find on a variety of stocks and bonds are Sir William Mackenzie and Fred Stark Pearson. The former made his name from railway construction and the latter was an electrical engineer with a keen desire to make and spend money. These two teamed up to build electric tramways in various parts of the world including Brazil, Mexico and Spain. They were joined by one of the most flamboyant financiers of the time, Alfred Lowenstein, a Belgian born trader of impressive style and insatiable need for wealth.

By fair means and foul Lowenstein raised ever increasing amounts of money for the Canadian companies (Brazilian Traction, Mexico Light & Power and the Barcelona Traction Company, to name but three), as well as controlling European artificial silk manufacture. His activities allowed him to accumulate a vast fortune, including 8 villas in Biarritz, and, it appears, several enemies. In 1928 he "fell" from his personal aircraft whilst flying between Britain and France. Despite a belief that such a fall could not have been accidental, the actual cause was never discovered.

Fred Stark Pearson was drowned (in less suspicious circumstances) when the Lusitania was torpedoed by a German submarine in 1915.

Barcelona Traction figured highly in the activities of Lowenstein and Pearson (whose facsimile signature appears on the bonds), and was also the subject of a famous case in international law following its nationalisation without compensation.

CHINA

The "discovery" of Chinese bonds by Drumm and Henseler in their book of 1976 was a major factor in the blossoming of scripophily. Not only were the bonds of known rarity, they were also attractive and even maintained a lingering quotation on the London Stock Exchange, thus giving the potential seller a guaranteed exit. Many early collectors began with Chinese material and within a few years saw some dramatic price swings. In 1979 a £500 bond issued by the Deutsche-Asiatische Bank in 1898 realised £14,000 at auction, a peak for the Chinese and one not since reached. The publication of a new and far more comprehensive catalogue, "China's Foreign Debt" by Kuhlmann in 1983 once again drew attention to this fascinating field for the collector.

Chinese bonds have always had an international appeal, a factor which stems from the long standing involvement of the "major powers" (Britain, Russia, France, Germany and the USA) in the politics and economy of the country. A brief history concentrating on the period which most interests scripophilists, namely 1895-1938, may be helpful.

THE NINETEENTH CENTURY

Throughout the nineteenth century Britain, Russia and France sought permanent bases in China. Whereas Russia was keen to establish an eastern seaboard (and ideally surround the country), Britain, France and later Germany, were intent on preserving the profitable trading outposts based largely on tea, silk and opium. Several land licences were granted, the main ones being Hong Kong to the British, Amur province as far south as Vladivostock to the Russians, and Indo-China (now Vietnam) to France.

Although in later years the continued presence of foreign governments led to some major uprisings there were also considerable benefits to the country, particularly with regard to industrialization and the development of its infrastructure. The 1870s saw the beginnings of industrial revolution and several government-supervised companies were established, but perhaps the most significant event was the first steam railway, opened in 1876.

The early development of railways is dealt with at some length later but it is interesting to note the political significance of railways and their impact on certain major events in Chinese history. The Russians, for example, sought to pressurize the country by building the Trans-Siberia Railway as close to the northern borders of China as possible with a view to annexing Mongolia, Manchuria and Korea. At a later date (1911) the revolution led by Sun Yat-sen to oust the Manchu government was sparked off by a government decision to take over all the country's main railways. A great many bonds were issued to finance railway construction and several examples are described later.

Seemingly endless land-grabbing by foreign governments resulted in the formation of a nationalist society popularly known as the "Boxers", although more correctly, 'The Society of Righteous Harmonious Fists'. The result of their uprising, culminating in the siege of foreign embassies in Peking in 1900, had the opposite effect to their objective. Foreign governments put down the revolt with an international force and resumed intervention in a rather more determined fashion.

THE TWENTIETH CENTURY

Continuing dissatisfaction with the Manchu Government's failure to curb foreign land-grabbing led to the formation of a major new revolutionary movement. Its leader was Dr Sun Yat-sen. By 1911, revolution had spread across the land and in February 1912 the last Emperor of China abdicated, making way for the Republic. This change of government is clearly highlighted in the wording on the

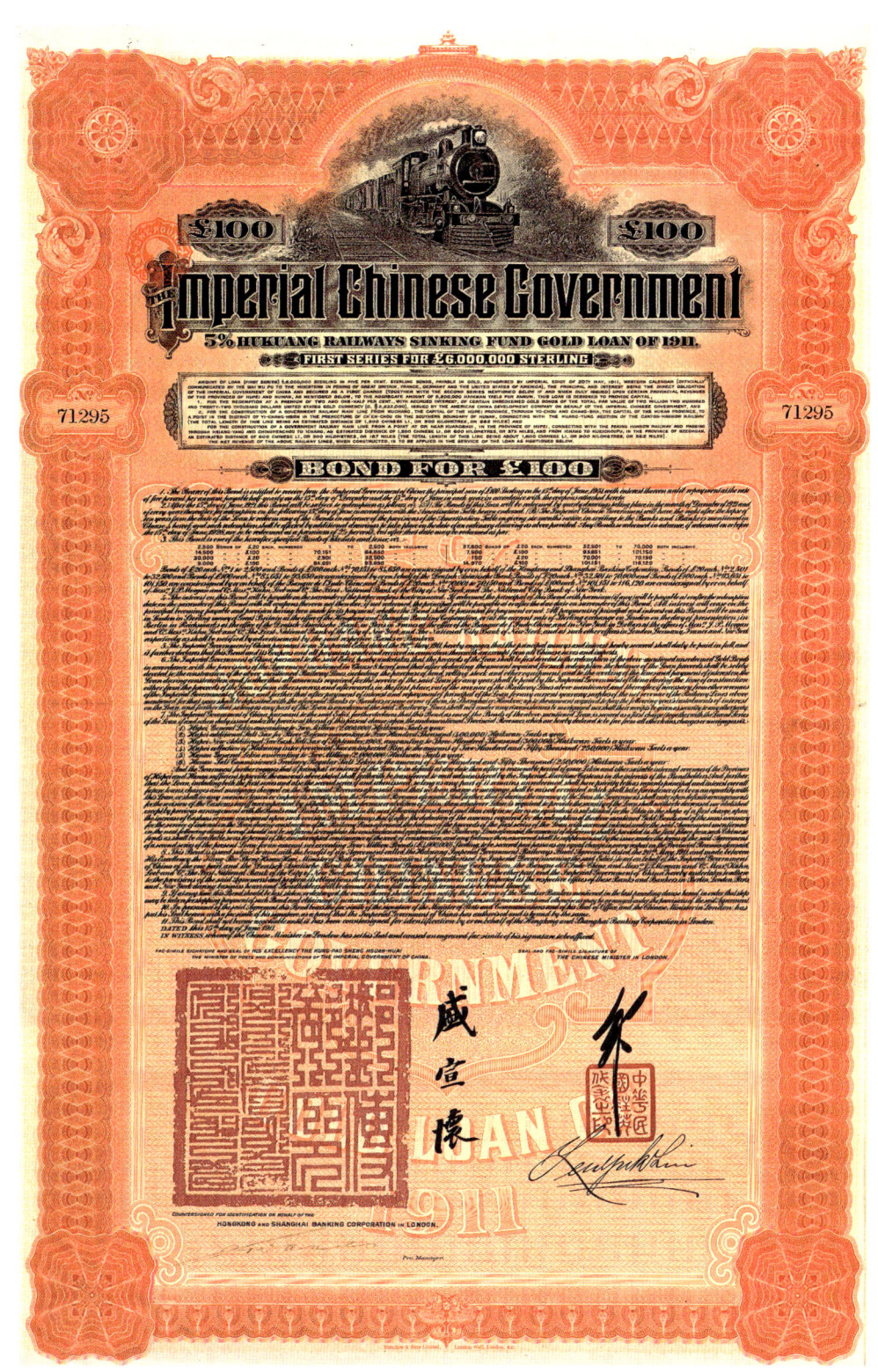

Bonds to finance the Hukuang Railway were the last to be issued by Imperial China's Manchu Dynasty. Four countries participated in the loan (England, France, Germany and the United States).

bonds themselves, which, prior to 1912 were issued 'by Imperial Edict' (as on the Hukuang Railway bonds of 1911, for example) but thereafter carried the words 'Republic of China'. One of the first issues to be so described was the 5% Gold Loan of 1912 (the "Crisp" Loan).

Sun Yat-sen did not have control of the military forces, however, and was forced to resign the presidency of the Republic in 1912. He moved to the south and formed the Nationalist Party (the "Kuomintang"). Uprisings were put down by the government which had anticipated civil war and under Yuan Shih-K'ai persuaded the major powers to pull together a £25 million foreign loan to finance military preparations and "reorganise government finances". It is interesting to see where the money went.

The 1913 Reorganisation Loan

The bonds were issued at 90% and out of this the banks received 6% for their work. The Chinese therefore started with only 84% of the total, namely £21m, of which £10m was used to settle other maturing debt, £5.5m to cover "current and extraordinary expenses of administration", £3m to pay the army, leaving only £1.5 for the "reorganisation of the Salt Administration" (the prime purpose of the loan!). This was one of the largest Chinese bond issues assembled by the major powers and incorporated stringent conditions of repayment. The issue was four times oversubscribed in Britain (which accounted for 30% of the total) and 5 times in Germany. The bonds, engraved by Waterlow are some of the most attractive of all Chinese items.

From Sun Yat-sen to Mao Tse-tung

Despite Sun Yat-sen's brief reign his portrait appears on several bonds, the most notable being the Shanghai-Hangchow-Ningpo Railway which was begun as early as 1907. The 1936 6% bonds were issued to finance completion of the project with the building of a bridge across the Chien Tang. The face of the bonds carries a portrait of Sun Yat-sen and the back bears a fine picture of the bridge which was completed in 1937, only seven days before being blown up by the Chinese Army as it retreated from the Japanese advance.

Sun Yat-sen fled the country coming under the powerful influence of the Bolsheviks, who sought to gain control of China through the Kuomintang. He died in 1925.

The new leader of the Kuomintang was Chiang Kai-shek, who had spent the previous two years being trained by the Soviet Union. Early military successes encouraged him to take a more adventurous line against the advice of his Russian advisers. He soon conquered the north, and shortly after, most of China. Nanking became the capital and Chiang Kai-shek married the daughter of one of Shanghai's richest bankers. By 1928 he had taken Peking.

Chiang's success upset the communists, who began to form a separate force under the leadership of Mao Tse-tung. Civil war was only deferred as a result of the attack from Japan in 1937 and it was at this time that China ceased payment on its foreign loans.

Four years after the Japanese war the Communists took full control and Chiang was expelled to Taiwan. Mao Tse-tung proclaimed the formation of the People's Republic of China on 1 October 1949 and all outstanding bonds remained in default.

The 1913 Reorganisation Loan was one of the largest issues by the Nationalist Government. Many of these bonds, which were finely engraved by Waterlow, are available today.

COLLECTING FIELDS

Chinese bonds fall into two major categories, the foreign loans issued by overseas banks to raise hard currency and the "internals". Most scripophilists interested in China have tended to concentrate on foreign bonds as it is these which are the most comprehensively catalogued. They are also the most attractive and easiest to read (text being usually in English, French or German). It is, however, a mistake to ignore the "internals".

The Internals

Every country raises funds by the issue of bonds in its own currency and China was no exception. Not all were repaid, however, and the authorities tended to view them more as taxes and an opportunity to defraud rather than a genuine offer of investment. Issues of internal bonds were grouped into three main periods:

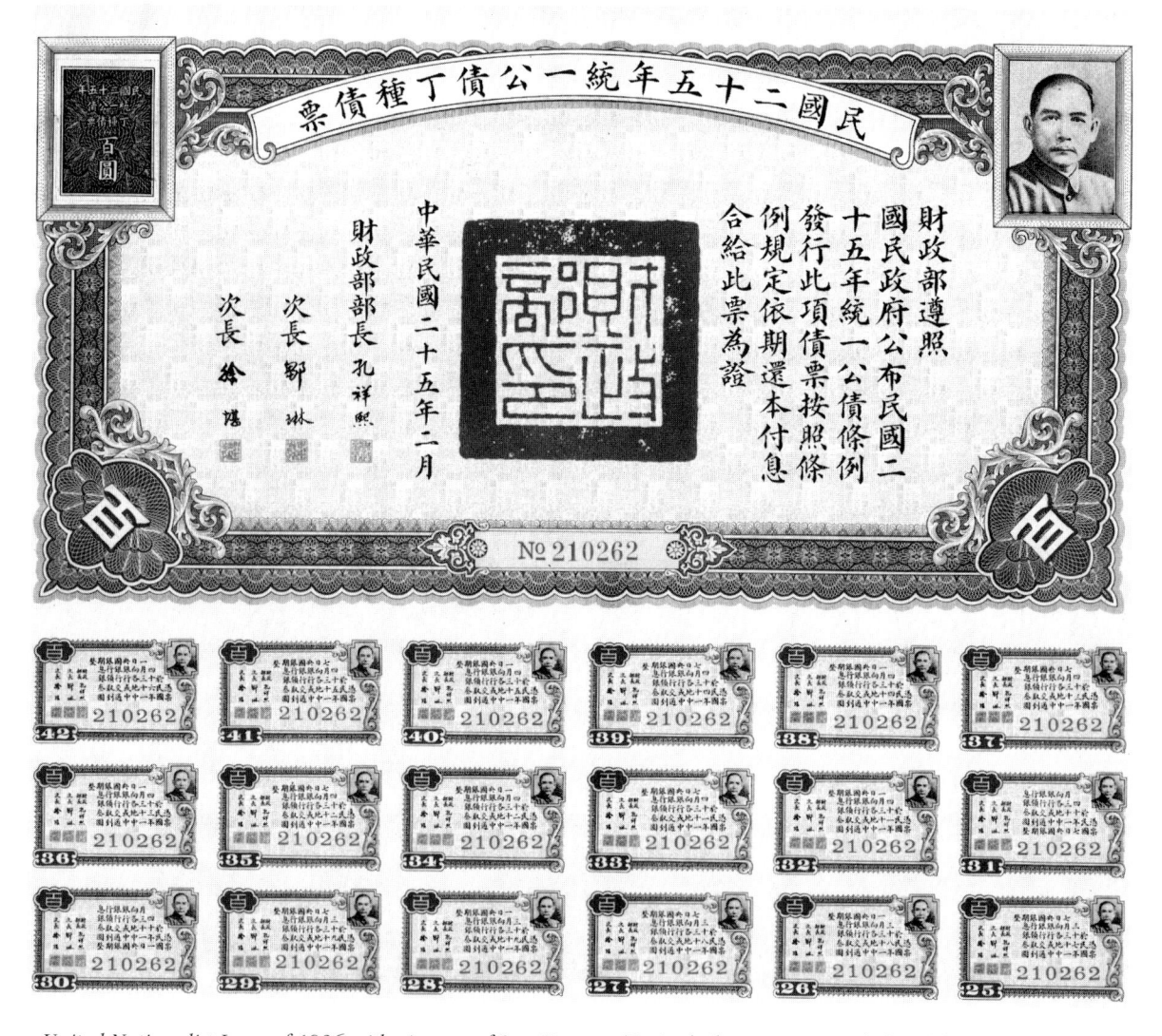

United Nationalist Loan of 1936 with vignette of Sun Yat-sen. Typical Chinese "internal" bond for Yuan 100.

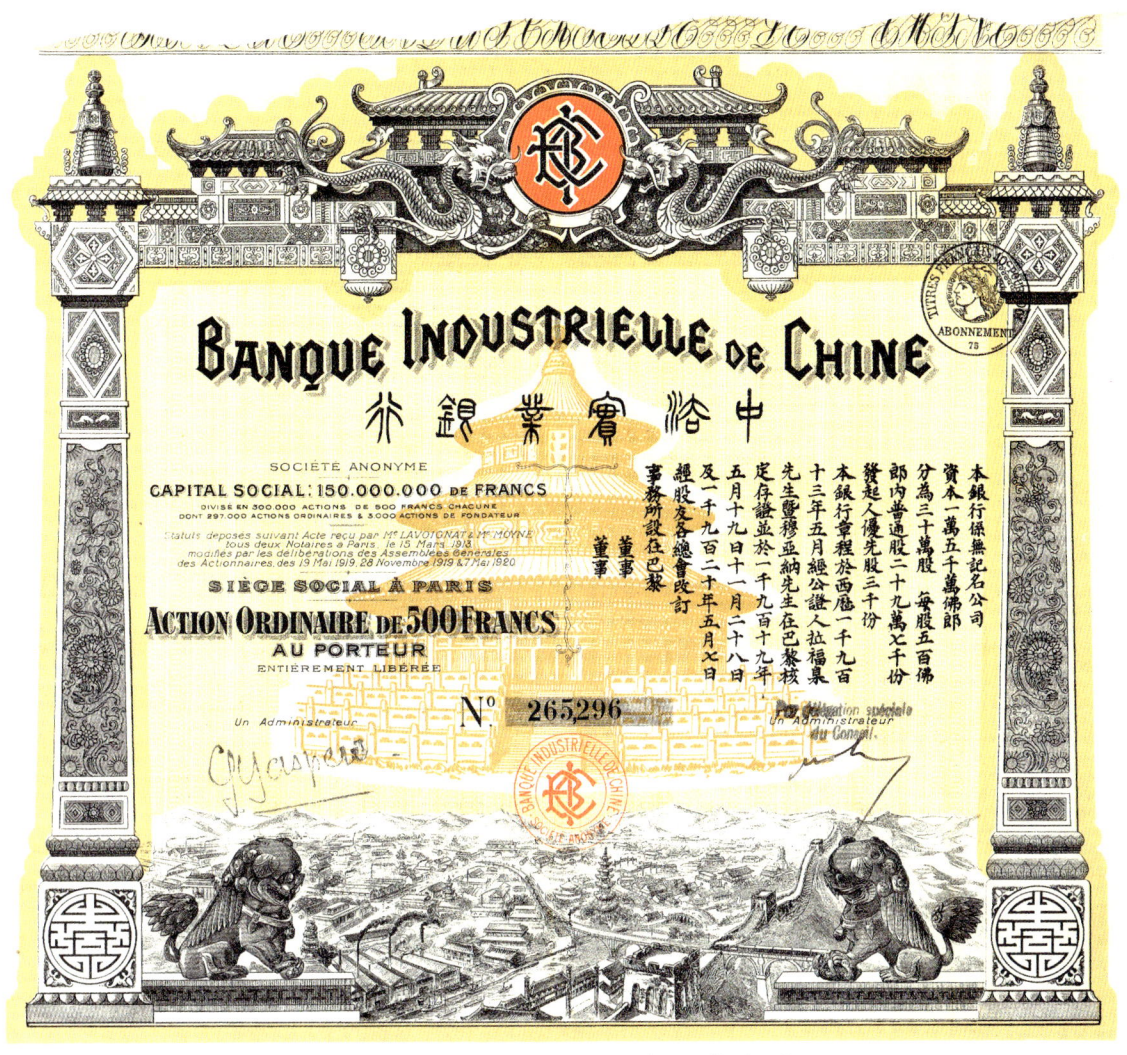

Set up as a rival to the Banque de L'Indo-Chine, the Banque Industrielle de Chine was active in many infrastructure projects. It certainly boasts one of the most attractive of all Chinese certificates.

1. The Imperial era. There were three major issues in 1894, 1898 and 1911, all of which are extremely rare.
2. The early years of the Republic. The first two issues, the 8% Military Loan and the 6% Consolidated Loan, were issued in 1912 but neither was a great success with the now more wary Chinese investor. Despite lack of local enthusiasm, National loans were issued in most years of the Republic.
3. The Second World War. Numerous domestic issues were launched in this period, many of which had no chance of repayment. The most commonly seen is the National Liberty Bond issue of 1937.

Internal bonds, especially the more common types can be purchased relatively cheaply. Most resemble banknotes, written in Chinese on their face and English on the back.

Foreign Bonds

These attractive bonds were issued and quoted on most major European stock markets usually following protracted negotiations between the Chinese and the Major Powers. Political interference was always at the highest level as the loans were not only seen as good business by the banks but also as a means of exerting continuous control over China by the West. The conditions attached to repayment were often onerous, imposing difficult obligations on the local population, a factor which greatly contributed to the anti foreign feelings of the Boxers and ultimately the Communists.

Fifty foreign loans are listed in Kuhlmann but not all are available to the collector as several were fully repaid and others have never been seen. Taking account of denominations and types, there are about 430 different foreign bonds. Prior to the 1987 Settlement there were about 2,600,000 individual Chinese foreign bonds outstanding, but many have been lost or destroyed over time.

Foreign bonds were issued to construct railways, finance Government debt or finance specific foreign purchases, such as aircraft.

Of the 50 issues, approximately 23 were concerned with railway financing, the largest being for the construction of the Lung-Tsing-U-Hai Railway.

THE LUNG-TSING-U-HAI RAILWAY

The Lung-Tsing-U-Hai was one of the longest railways in the country and its story is typical of many of the lines built with foreign assistance.

Discussions between the National Assembly and the Belgian Compagnie General de Chemins de Fer et de Tramways en Chine led to the signing of a loan agreement in September 1912 for £10 million. The purpose was to construct a major railway from Kansu to the sea. Two main sections were involved, the Pieulo and the Lo'tung.

The former ran between Loyang and Kaifeng and had been built by the Belgian Compagnie Générale in 1905 and financed by a Belgian loan raised in 1903 and subsequently repaid by the 1913 £10 million loan. In order to block further Belgian concessions, the acting Governor of Honan established the Lo'tung Railway Company, which had the objective of constructing four major railways in the province linking up to form the Lo'tung section. Various methods were used to finance these sections, for example owners of more than 50 mu (about one-seventh of an acre) had to buy a 5 Ti share for every 50 mu, and businesses with a capital of over 300 Taels had to buy one share, over 500 Taels, two shares, etc. Other more exotic pressures were exerted, such as surtaxes on salt and agricultural production, and a levy of 0.12 silver dollars on each ounce of opium produced.

But progress was slow, and increasing local dissatisfaction led to riots, the most serious being the burning down of the company office at Huayin, together with local schools and telegraph poles — symbols of exploitation of the poor. Eventually the Government took overall control in 1911.

The enormity of the project meant that additional funds were required to complete the railroad and new bonds were issued in 1920, 1921, 1923 and 1925.

THE 1987 REPAYMENT

Quite unexpectedly but following considerable diplomatic pressure by the British Government, the Peoples Republic of China ("PRC") were prevailed upon to settle outstanding claims by British holders of Chinese bonds and those whose assets had been confiscated following their expulsion from China in 1948.

During 1987 a fund of £20 million was made available by the PRC to settle all claims and at the time of the announcement it was felt that this would result in a 5-8% payout on the bonds face value assuming around 30-40% of all outstanding bonds were lodged for settlement. In fact rather less than 10% were submitted thus resulting in a final payout of 62.25% of the face value. Thus there are still

This was the first bond issue under the Chinese National Government in 1912. The issue was organised by London stockbrokers C. Birch Crisp & Co. and is often described as the "Crisp Loan".

The Compagnie Générale de Chemins de Fer et de Tramways en Chine was an active financier and contractor of Chinese railways.

Founded in 1890, Allianz Versicherung AG is now Germany's largest insurance company. The company originated in Bavaria under the strong influence of Baron von Finck of Merck, Finck & Co., bankers.

over 2 million bonds available to collectors! A large number but a misleading one as over 50% of these are accounted for by the 1913 Reorganisation and the 1925 Boxer issues. Several other issues are extremely rare and may be expensive to acquire.

FRANCE

France has some of the most attractive certificates in the world. Most readily available material dates from around 1900, although early pieces can be obtained. Fine examples are shares in the Canal de Richelieu (1753) and the Mine de Plomb Tenant Argent à Lenards (1790). In order to provide a better understanding of French material, a brief history of the economic development of the country follows.

HISTORICAL BACKGROUND

The Industrial Revolution began in Britain around the 1770s but did not reach France until after the end of the Napoleonic wars in 1815 and even then it was not until about 1830 that real progress in industrialization got under way.

The eighteenth century was broken up by wars and the 1789 Revolution, thus inhibiting the development of industry. The population was widely spread

Not THE Claridges, but a French Hotel group whose share certificates, if nothing else, were outstanding examples of dramatic art.

over the countryside and in 1700 only three towns (Paris, Lyons and Marseilles) exceeded 100,000. Great emphasis was placed on family-owned and run companies and little encouragement was provided by external financing bodies. The State's finances were in a mess, a situation tailor made for John Law.

John Law

Law was a Scottish immigrant, forced to leave England following a successful, albeit illegal, duel. He developed an economic theory based on the belief that the unrestricted issue of money by a Central Bank would provide continuous stimulus to the economy. He was of course absolutely right, but the inevitable hyper-inflation proved a counter to success! However, it was some time before the effects of his policies were apparent and in that time he managed to persuade Louis XIV to give him virtual carte blanche over the French economy. His first requirement, the establishment of a central bank responsible for taxation and public debt was implemented in 1716 and in the following year he gained exclusive rights to exploit France's Colonies through a commercial company, "Compagnie d'Occident". This company absorbed several existing trading concerns, such as the French East India Company ("Compagnie des Indes") and the Santo Domingo Company. Law became collector of taxes and controller of the Royal Mint as well as holder of the tobacco monopoly and manager of the African slave trade. On a more personal front he also gained exclusive rights to develop France's interests in Louisiana through the "Mississippi Company". His apparent success in the public sector gave him the aura of a financial guru and shares in his Mississippi Company rocketed from Livres 500 to 18,000, however, hopes of discoveries of gold and silver failed to materialise. The venture soon collapsed causing a major financial crisis and his forced emigration of the country. By the end of the eighteenth century France was on the verge of bankruptcy, largely due to the efforts of John Law.

Later Developments

Domestic industrialization may have been slow in the eighteenth century, but foreign trade certainly was not and business with the colonies and continental partners thrived. Textiles, the refining of sugar and vegetable oils and the manufacture of cheap trinkets for the purchase of slaves were all active businesses — at least until the Revolution.

In 1808 three types of company were created; the joint company (owner-managed and financed), the limited company (externally financed) and the joint-stock company.

Of these, the most common was the first and the most unusual the last. Regulations restricting joint-stock companies were so rigid, at least until 1867 (largely thanks to the John Law episode) that between 1815 and 1848 only 342 such companies were formed. This explains the dearth of early share certificates available for today's collector of French commercial enterprises. Those joint-stock companies formed were largely in the areas of coal mining, metallurgy, chemicals and textiles. One of the largest companies of the time (Creusot) was a 'limited' company.

Finance was mainly internally generated by each company although during the 1840s and 1850s numerous bond issues were made by companies, such as Decarzeville in 1842, to finance replacement machinery.

French road transport was good, even during the eighteenth century, and an effective canal system was developed during the early part of the next. Railways were only used for carrying coal from the

A fine example of a share specifically designed to match the location. Surely the ultimate in "Gothic Scripophily"! The company is believed to have dredged the bay around Mont St Michel off northern France — an island connected to the mainland at low tide.

mines to waiting barges and it was not until 1837 that the first passenger service was opened between Paris and St. Germain. For comparison, in 1848 France had 1,800 km of railways while Britain, Germany and Belgium each exceeded 10,000 km. But once building was under way progress was fast and there is no doubt that the growth of the railways greatly assisted the growth of heavy industry. As will be apparent from the later chapter on Automobiles, France led the world in the early commercial manufacture of vehicles around the turn of the century.

As a result of huge compensation payments made by France after the 1870/1 Franco-Prussian War, investment opportunities were in great demand in Germany. Several "scams" resulted as new companies were repeatedly sold at higher and higher prices until they were offered to the public. Bau-Gesellschaft für Eisenbahn-Unternehmungen was one such company, full of promise but devoid of assets.

CERTIFICATES FOR THE COLLECTOR

There is a shortage of early industrial material, however, some early certificates which are fairly readily available are the Royal Loans or "Rentes" of the seventeenth and eighteenth centuries. These are described more fully on page 92.

There were many companies formed towards the end of the nineteenth century particularly those which were transport related. Some of these were only concerned with domestic business whilst others directed their attention overseas. Many of these shares and also those issued around the turn of the century are attractive often having been designed by well known artists of the time.

One feature of French and Belgian shares which the collector will notice is the wavy cut down one side or top of a certificate. This is not a sign of damage. The stub of the certificate which would be retained by the issuing company has been separated using an unevenly shaped wavy rule, thus enabling, at some future date, the possibility of verifying authenticity of the share by matching it up to its stub. A crude but effective anti forgery device.

Types of Certificates

The difference between "bonds" and "shares" was explained earlier. Certificates issued in France (and in other Continental European countries) use different terminology and have additional variations which the collector should be aware of. In translation, the terms "registered" and "bearer" become "nominative" and "au porteur", respectively and it is interesting to note that as most French (and other European) shares were issued in bearer form, registered (or "nominative") material is appre-

ciably scarcer. Other variations/translations are summarised below:
- "Action". Ordinary share. Similar word to that used in other countries such as Aktie (Germany), Azioni (Italy), or Accione (Spain).
- "Part de Fondateur". More usually referred to as a Founders Share. These were only issued at the time of a company's formation and distributed free to the original founders entitling them to a fixed supplementary dividend. They also carried voting rights.
- "Action de Dividende". Once again, only issued at time of formation. Entitled the owner to receive dividends but had no capital or voting rights.
- "Action de Jouissance". Literal translation is a "share of enjoyment"! These shares had the added interest of being periodically drawn by lot for capital repayment but still continuing to provide the holder with dividends.
- "Obligation". Bond.

GERMANY

Over recent years the scripophily market in Germany has grown enormously and it is now one of the largest and most active in the world. The market is serviced by a large number of dealers and auction houses with interest centred on German material but still a wide ranging enthusiasm for all things historical irrespective of source country.

SUMMARY HISTORY

Germany lagged behind both Britain and France in industrialization largely due to the diversity of the country (national unification was not achieved until 1871) and its geographical location which resulted in regular involvement in European wars. Additionally, its transport systems were poor until well into the nineteenth century.

Until the arrival of steam traction, there was little industry and the population was ninety per cent rural. The position changed rapidly after the building of the first railway from Nurnberg to Furth in 1835. This short line was followed by the longer Leipzig-Dresden Railway in 1839 and during the 1840s over 100 million Talers were invested in shares and debentures of the railway companies. Among the many lines constructed, the major ones were:

Munich-Augsburg	1840
Cologne-Aachen	1843
Berlin-Hamburg	1846
Cologne-Minden	1847

All were privately controlled, although the Prussian government subsidized approximately half of the total investment. The greatest benefit of the lines was the improved transport of coal, thus generating further industry, particularly on the large coal and iron fields. Between 1850 and 1875 most railway companies were purchased by the State for economic or strategic reasons.

Development of an infrastructure was not limited to railways, and both canals and roads were constructed. Many of the new roads were owned privately and operated a toll system (very like the US 'turnpikes'); an example is the Mecklenburg-Strelitz road, which continued to charge users until 1915.

"Thuringia", more correctly known as Eisenbahn und Allgemeine Rück-Versicherungs-Gesellschaft Thuringia, is still one of Germany's foremost insurance companies. The founders' share shown, dated 1853, is believed unique and certainly ranks as one of the most beautiful German certificates.

Early shares are fairly scarce but some fine pieces appear at auction from time to time, an example being a certificate for 11.5 shares in the "Banque Priviliegiée & Garantie à Poll & Panheel" issued in Cologne and dated 1792. Prior to national unification in 1871 bonds were issued by many of the independent states. In 1789, for example there were as many as 314 such states so it not surprising that their rulers often ran out of funds.

Most of Germany's commerce was domestic and it was not until the latter part of the nineteenth century that much attention was paid to international trade. At that time several banks were formed to encourage such expansion, for example the Deutsch-Asiatische Bank in 1889, and the Deutsche-Uberseebank in 1886. The major German banks, such as Deutsche Bank and Dresdener Bank, were formed in the early 1870s, and a close relationship with industry developed from a very early date. This close involvement continues to the present day and involves both lending and equity participation.

Deutsche Bank is today the most famous of Germany's commercial banks. Most pre-war shares were exchanged for new shares denominated in Deutsche Mark after the war. Earlier uncancelled shares like this are rare.

The most significant date in recent history is 1871, for not only was Germany 'unified' but it also standardized its currency. Until that date, seven different silver currencies, based on Taler or Gulden, existed. These were eventually replaced by the Gold Mark when Germany joined Britain in adopting the gold standard. These currency changes are clearly reflected in the bonds and shares of the period.

LATER DEVELOPMENTS AND CERTIFICATES

Following the intensive period of industrial growth, the end of the nineteenth century saw the building of many towns, together with the associated services of electricity, tramways and retail businesses. Many shares existing today bear witness to this growth.

A great many bonds were issued by cities and states in the nineteenth century, some in less numbers than others, but most are decorative and highly sought after.

Among the most wanted German shares now are the early pieces issued by the giant industrial concerns of today, such as Siemens, Krupp, Mannesmann, BASF and Daimler-Benz. Zoo shares also are always in demand and always expensive!

Several dollar and sterling loans were issued between the First and Second World Wars. Some, such as the Young and Dawes loans were arranged by the United States Government to assist in the rebuilding of Germany, whilst others were specifically issued by cities or companies. During the Second World War a batch of these bonds were reputed to have been stolen and as a result anyone seeking to redeem his dollar bond must prove long standing ownership. There are large holdings of

Siemens & Halske AG was founded in 1897 by the Siemens family and Deutsche Bank. This share of 1942 portrays Werner von Siemens and an early telegraph machine.

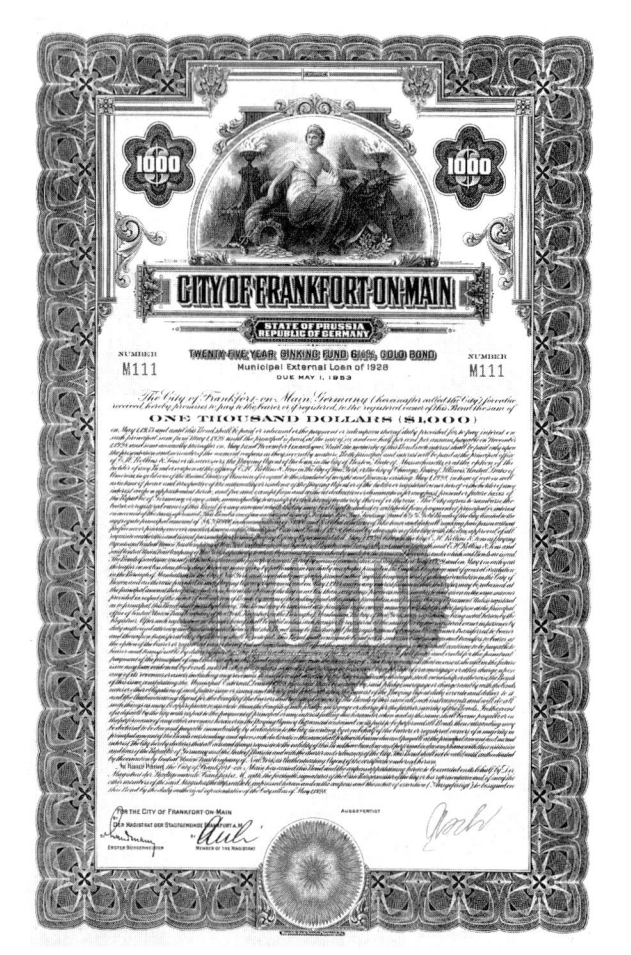

Typical US dollar bond issued to help rebuild Germany during the 1920s and 1930s. This one is for the City of Frankfurt.

these bonds around the world and many attempts are made to use the bonds as security. Bankers beware!

Two other issues deserve mention, these are sterling bonds issued by the "Free State of Saxony" and the "City of Dresden" in 1927. Both issues are in default at time of writing but a settlement is expected at some stage.

BELGIUM

Well-endowed with enormous reserves of coal and iron combined with the presence of a natural waterway system, Belgium was able to take full and speedy advantage of the industrial revolution. The first limited company was formed in 1835, only four years after the country's foundation, known as "S.A. Hauts Fournaux, Usines et Charbonnage de Marcinelle et Couillet", it was a vast organization involved in iron and coal mining. Another equally large enterprise, which continues to this day, is "John Cockerill S.A.". The Cockerill brothers, Scottish emigrés, bought the castle at Seraing in 1814 and built one of the largest and most modern metallurgical plants in Europe. Locomotives, textile machinery and marine engines were produced but following the creation of the Belgian State, Dutch funding was reduced and by 1841, the formal Belgian company was formed to place the operation on a sound and long lasting financial footing. Original shares appear rarely at auction. However, business activity in the land we now know as Belgium goes back well before this date.

During the fourteenth century Bruges dominated the European credit market acting as a clearing house for all kinds of financial transactions. The Medici Bank became one of the foremost lenders to European royalty but by 1530 Antwerp had become the single most important financial centre of the World.

The reason for Antwerp's importance was quite simply lack of inhibiting regulations and a merchant dominated environment. As well as trade related instruments, such as bills of exchange and commodity contracts, Antwerp established a major bond market with issues by most European Governments trading on the Exchange built in 1531. But revolution in 1566 ended the city's dominance and business moved to its main rival, Amsterdam.

It is the more recent period since the early 1800's which has most interest for scripophilists. The major banks of Société General and Banque Belge often took controlling interests in companies of the time, leaving only small shareholdings in the hands of the general public. The company 'La Providence' for example had only ten to twenty outside shareholders. Foreign capital was supplied by the Rothschilds and others, and intense business activity soon established Belgium as one of the foremost industrial countries of Europe. Plans for the construction of the first and most concentrated railway network in the world were presented as early as 1830 and it was not long before Belgium became a major exporter of railway equipment and tramways, as is evidenced by the many bearer shares seen today.

Textiles had for many years been an important industry, but with the arrival of steam the business was more actively developed. Initially drawing ideas and equipment from Britain (indeed, Lievin Bauwens imported a whole factory, including workers), but the natural innovation and inventiveness of the people soon improved production techniques.

Only two German sterling loans remain in default, the City of Dresden and this one of the Free State of Saxony.

Many of the share certificates available to collectors relate to the basic industries of coal, iron and textiles, but many others exist, particularly the early railway and canal companies and some of the more unusual such as those issued to finance the Zoos of Brussels, Antwerp and Ghent. As well as shares issued to finance the home industries and develop colonial interests, the most notable of these being those based in the Congo (Zaire).

HOLLAND

Considering the proximity of Belgium and Holland, it is perhaps surprising how widely they differ. Industrial Revolution came late to Holland and whereas Belgium was able to build on substantial mineral resources and a long history of industrialization, Holland was quite the opposite with most of its businessmen traditionally involved in shipping and commerce.

A prime example of close Belgian and British association in the textile industry. Fine looking and rare share issued in 1853 by the Anglo Belgian Patent Flax Wool & Cotton Company.

Mention has already been made of the dominance of Amsterdam in world financial markets following the demise of Antwerp but it was the formation of the Dutch East India Company (Vereenigde Oost Indische Compagnie) which is perhaps the most famous reminder of the influence of the country on foreign trade and colonization.

The Company was formed in 1602 and its shares and those of the Dutch West India Company became actively traded on the world's first stock market opened in Amsterdam in 1634. The East India Company dominated Dutch business and lasted for almost 200 years. During its life it employed 500,000 people and built 1,500 ships, but wars with Britain and Britain's eventual control of the Cape of Good Hope and Ceylon, led to its collapse in 1799. Shareholders were issued with receipts for their investment rather than share certificates and such pieces are both scarce and expensive.

So far as 'industrial' companies are concerned the only contenders, even by 1803, were a rifle factory at Kuilerburg, a textile business at Amsterdam, a glass works at Leerdam and fourteen sugar beet factories. Sugar refining and diamond cutting were the two early industries of any significance, the latter being established in Amsterdam in 1822.

Railway construction was slow, and in 1850 the country could only boast 170 km of track versus Belgium's 861 km. The first line was built between Amsterdam and Haarlem in 1839, more emphasis being placed on waterways and shipping.

Early Dutch certificates are relatively scarce as it was not until 1863 that limited liability companies were authorized by the Government. Those items which do exist are of primary interest to the local market.

Zoo shares are always popular and those of the Brussels Zoo, particularly so.

GREAT BRITAIN

Some background to the development of London as a financial centre has already been provided in Part 1 and further history on early company activity such as the South Sea Company and the formation of the Bank of England is covered on Page 89. This section will mainly concentrate on more recent events beginning with the Industrial Revolution.

THE INDUSTRIAL REVOLUTION

Despite the frenzied industrial activity of France and Belgium, there is little doubt that the Industrial Revolution began in Britain. An exact date is difficult to specify, but economic historians tend to agree on a period around the 1770s-1780s. The forty years or so prior to this period prepared the ground and three principal contributory factors have been identified:
1. The development of international markets, particularly through colonialisation and improved reliability of shipping transportation.
2. A period of unusually good agricultural harvests.
3. An increase in overall population.

The catalysts required to convert these factors into "revolution" took the form of a burst of inventions together with the construction of roads and canals. The inventions, such as Arkwright's water frame, Hargreave's Spinning Jenny and Watt's steam engine, had an enormous effect on the cotton and iron industries and it was the latter which previously had been suffering from lack of fuel (having relied on local forests) which was able to benefit most from improved transport enabling cheaper deliveries of coal to steel areas. Thus Coalbrookdale's Iron Bridge became a milestone in the progress of industry. Built in 1779, the bridge was the first cast iron construction of its kind.

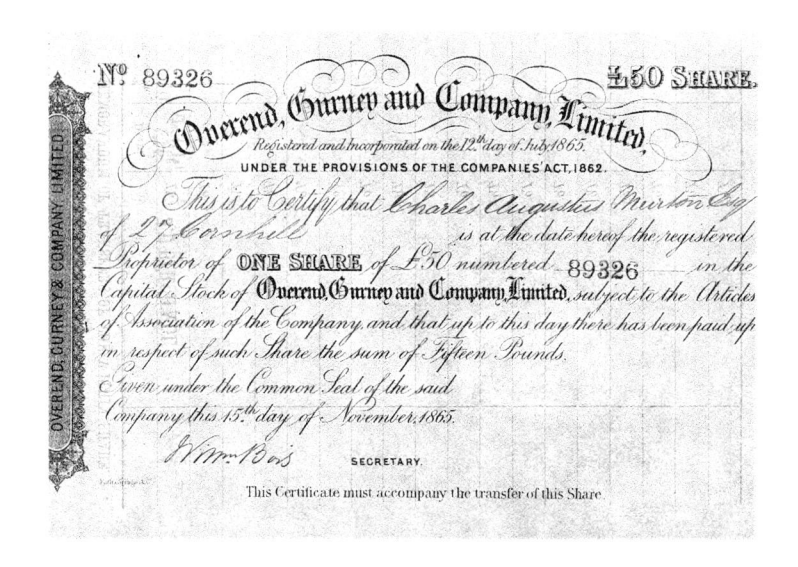

By 1760, as many as seventeen coke blast furnaces existed in the country and in the latter part of the eighteenth century the urban population ratio increased from sixteen to twenty-five per cent. There is no doubt that Britain benefited from the political revolutions going on in Europe and the United States, permitting it to consolidate an already powerful international economic position. All this despite the near financial disasters arising from "unfortunate" lending to South America and the activities of unscrupulous financial fraudsters. The powerful families of Rothschild and Baring played major roles in stabilising the big "crashes" during the early part of the nineteenth century, thus paving the way for a long period of progress beginning with the building of the railways.

Overend & Gurney became the first and largest discount house in England. Formed as a joint stock company in 1865 to shore up its finances, the company crashed a year later, resulting in a major run on London banks. As a result the whole concept of limited liability was brought into disrepute for many years to come.

Opened in 1825 the Stockton & Darlington was the world's first commercial steam railway. The preference share shown here was issued in 1858 and includes a fine quality vignette of the line.

RAILWAY DEVELOPMENT

It was not until 1825 that the world's first commercial railway was opened, running between Stockton and Darlington, but the greatest expansion occurred in the "mania" periods of 1836-7 and post-1850. In 1843, 2,000 miles of track existed and by 1867 this had risen to over 12,000 miles. Not only did the railway companies take away the trade of the old Turnpike Trusts and Canal Companies (by 1865 one-third of all canals were under the direct control of the railway companies), but they permitted a rapid expansion in industrialization. Associated businesses supplying rails, bricks and equipment all thrived, generating an enormous injection of funds into the economy.

The increased mobility of resources of labour and capital completely transformed the country. On the "negative" side, the redistribution of wealth prompted the Duke of Wellington to complain that railways "enabled the lower orders to go uselessly wandering about the country".

Initial collector enthusiasm for early railway shares has shown little abatement over the years and the subject retains its popularity. There were a great many British railway companies formed during the nineteenth century, most of which were controlled by relatively small groups of investors, thus limiting the initial number of originally issued share certificates. The availability of material is further hampered by the groupings of the early twentieth century and eventual nationalization. As a result of this process, most certificates were handed in to the head offices, such as Great Northern and Great Western. Initially these were no doubt kept in registers but over time many have been lost, spoiled, destroyed or at best, heavily overstamped "cancelled".

Despite this, certificates are available and the collector can have great fun building up a collection at sensible prices.

COMPANY FINANCING

Following the collapse of the South Sea Company in 1720 the Government, through the passing of the 'Bubble Act', prohibited the formation of joint-stock limited liability companies unless specifically authorized by Act of Parliament. This position continued until the limited liability acts of the 1850s and greatly restricted the number of such companies formed during that period. Not all were put off by the lengthy process of authorization, however, but such companies were largely limited to the Turnpike Trusts and Canal Companies. As a result, many small savers invested in canal shares, which around the 1790s experienced a boom.

The next change in legislation affecting limited liability companies did not come until the beginning of the twentieth century when further easing of the rules resulted in the formation of numerous ventures, many with exotic sounding names and little else.

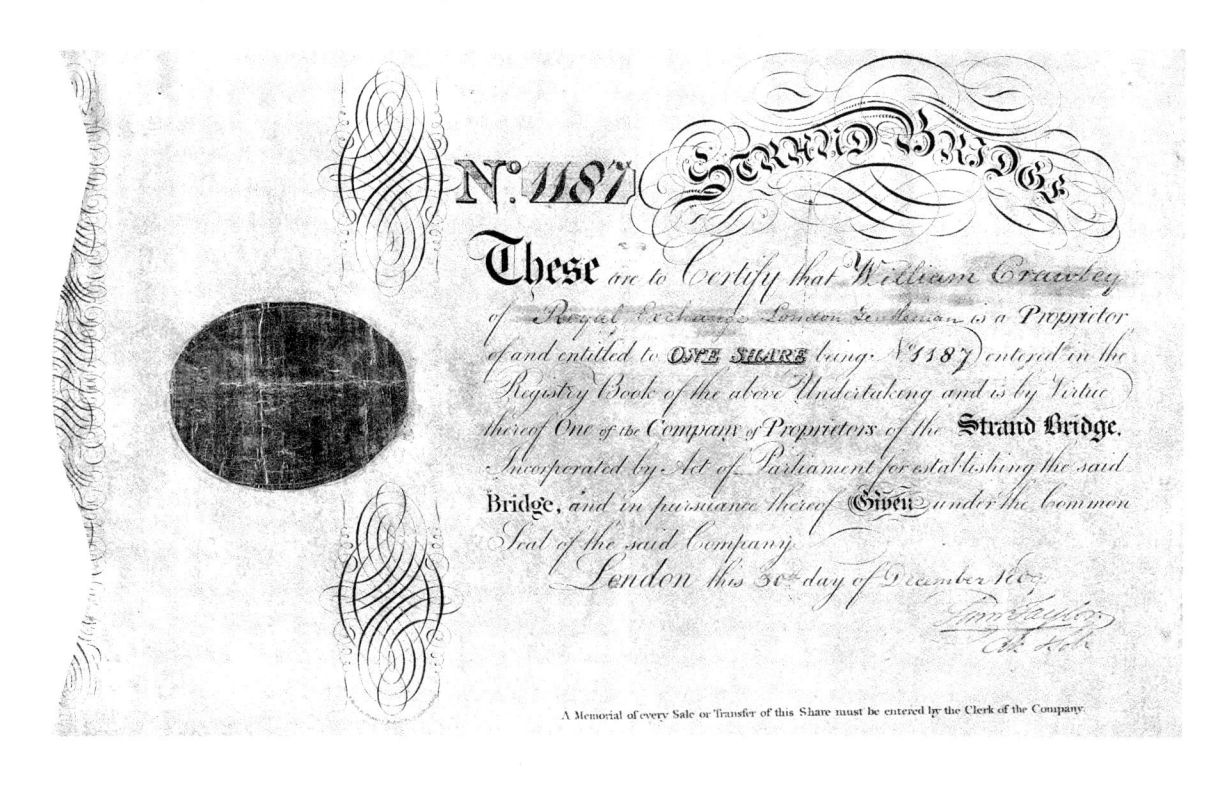

The Strand Bridge was built between 1811 and 1817 and was opened by the Prince Regent (the future King George IV) on the second anniversary of the Battle of Waterloo. It was consequently renamed "Waterloo". The original bridge was demolished in 1936 and its replacement opened in 1942. The share certificates are printed on vellum.

Few British certificates can match Colt Gun for dramatic impact!

COLLECTING GREAT BRITAIN

Railways are not the only worthwhile collecting theme within Great Britain. Indeed, there are many companies formed to build bridges, theatres, libraries and sporting facilities which offer the collector a wide variety of high-quality material. Many of these institutions were financed by small groups of local businessmen and the certificates can be attractive, bearing vignettes and fine seals, sometimes printed on vellum.

More recent material comes from all kinds of industrial enterprises. Such as:

Banking	Mining	Automobiles	Gas	Shipping
Publishing	Piers	Cemeteries	Libraries	Coal
Insurance	Theatre	Sport		

Prices of Victorian shares are remarkably low, probably due to lack of research and investigation, but also in some part, due to the relatively plain appearance of many English shares which contrast markedly with equivalent contemporary material from the USA and Continental Europe.

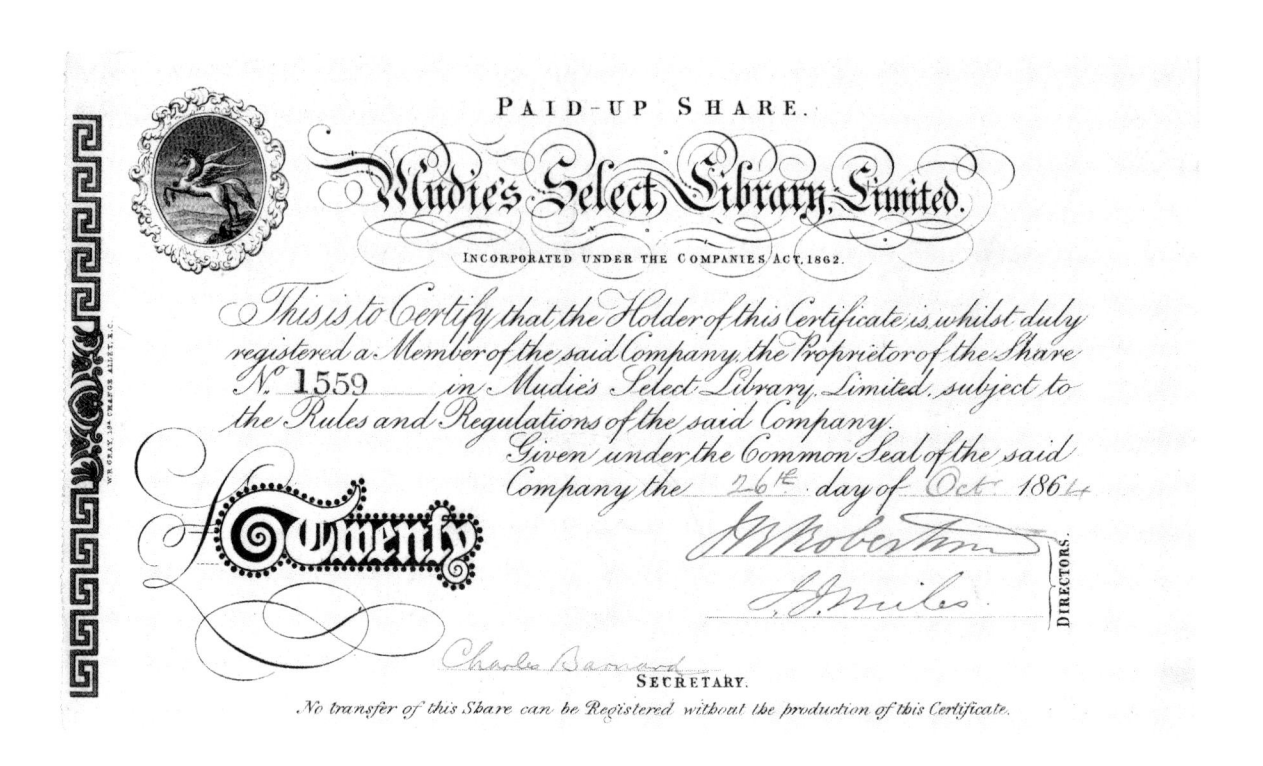

Mudie's Library had an enormous impact on the style and content of Victorian novels. The objective was to lend as many books as possible for a fee. Short novels were of no interest to Mudie who liked to divide a long one into two or three volumes, thus increasing revenue. The share certificates, like many English pieces were designed to resemble a bank note thus adding credibility.

RUSSIA

The 1991 break-up of the Soviet Union resulted in the formation of 12 independent states in addition to those of Estonia, Latvia and Lithuania. This event has provided the collector with the opportunity for increased specialisation within the general and simplified classification of "Russia".

Early Industrial Development

The sheer vastness of the country with its multi-lingual and multi-religious peoples added considerable delays to the coming of the industrial revolution to Russia. Development was further hindered by the effects of serfdom. Russia's eventual defeat in the Crimean War (1853-6) emphasized its economic and social backwardness. Following this, considerable efforts were made, especially by Tsar Nicolas I, to eliminate serfdom, and the Peasants Land Bank was set up in 1882 to assist in the transfer of land from the nobility. The 1870s saw a rapid development of railways and the start of oil exploration at Baku.

By the end of the century a major metallurgical industry was established in the Ukraine based on the ore of Krivoy Rog and the coal of the Donetz basin. The Tsar was instrumental in establishing the industry by recruiting a Welsh engineer named John Hughes to recreate the steel town of Merthyr Tydfil (Wales) in the Donbass. The formation of the New Russia Company in 1869 laid the foundations for the steel town initially named "Hughesovka" and later Donetz. The company's main product was rails, but it also specialised in armaments and munitions. John Hughes built and ran Hughesovka complete with hospital and school until his death in 1889. His sons took over but Hughesovka became a centre of drunkeness and anarchy and by the time of the 1917 Revolution the Hughes family were happy to leave. It was 1970 before the company was finally liquidated.

In 1897 Russia adopted the gold standard, thus encouraging foreign investors. The French and Belgians primarily invested in the metallurgical industries of the south, while Britain concentrated on oil and Germany on electricity. Share certificates and bonds of the period clearly reflect this internationally segregated development.

A Waterlow engraved debenture of the New Russia Company issued in 1910 well after John Hughes had established his replica of Merthyr Tydfil in the Ukraine.

SIGNIFICANCE TO SCRIPOPHILY

In order to appreciate the significance of Russia to the scripophilist, it is necessary to understand the enormity of the default which occurred in 1917 following the Revolution.

The overall lack of internal technological expertise combined with a social structure little changed from the Middle Ages meant that development could only come with the aid of foreigners, both technocrats and financiers. Creating an infrastructure from nothing and catering for the consequent shift in demographic behaviour, with peasants moving from the fields to towns, required vast amounts of capital.

At the time of default (1917) well over £1 billion in foreign bonds was outstanding and a similar amount of foreign equity in Russian companies. This position remained unchanged until 1986 when a surprise announcement from the governments of Britain and the USSR announced a settlement for bond holders and other claimants. Until that time Russia held the number one slot in the league of bad debtors.

The 1986 Settlement

Despite their default in 1917, Russian foreign bonds continued to be quoted on world stock markets, largely in the hope that one day a settlement would be agreed. Stock market prices over the years tended to move between 2-10% of face value although the early days of scripophily (around 1978-80) saw these levels well exceeded as market prices responded to collector demand. On 17th July 1986 their London listing was cancelled.

.The cause of cancellation was an agreement signed between the USSR and Britain to allow money which once belonged to the Imperial Russian Government and was frozen in Britain in 1917 to be used to settle claims by British nationals against Russia. The amount of money available for settlement was £46 million and depending on the number and amount of claims, a proportional settlement

The State Loan of 1909 was one of the largest Imperial Russian Government bond issues. At the time of default, the whole issue of £55 million was still outstanding.

was agreed. Initial estimates suggested 10% of face value but it soon became apparent that far less bonds than expected were being submitted and the calculation of applicable exchange rates at the time of default severely restricted the amount which other injured parties could claim. It is interesting to remember that at the time of the Revolution there were a great many foreign families living in Russia, often in great style and heavily involved in running the country's industry. These people were expelled from their homes and many who survive today have harrowing and fascinating tales to tell of their escape. They lost everything.

The final payout was 54.78% of the face value of bonds submitted. Out of the estimated 10-20 million bonds in existence only 1 million were handed in. Other countries continue to hope for a similar settlement for their citizens, but the break up of the USSR limits the chances.

Many Russian bonds were issued and held outside of Britain so it is not surprising that so few found their way to the Bank of England's incinerator. But many of those which were submitted were the sterling bonds issued to finance railways and cities. Some of these issues were already small and the settlement has had a marked effect on their current rarity. Examples are as follows:

Description	Bond Den.	Issued	Submitted
CITIES			
1913 City of St Petersberg	£100	14500	4506
1908 City of Moscow	£ 20	59778	16430
1912 City of Nicolaiev (1st)	£500	261	89
1910 City of Baku	£500	285	87
1909 City of Saratov	£100	4092	1194
RAILWAYS			
1912 Kahetian	£ 20	20000	4877
1910 Kokand Namangan	£100	2400	355
1911 Black Sea Kuban	£500	400	79
1910 Troitzk	£ 20	8798	1309

Bond Types for the Collector

Russian bonds fall into three main categories, State loans, railways and cities. A further category is the large number of companies, usually overseas ventures set up to develop the country. Most were privately owned and were ruined as a consequence of the Revolution.

Over sixty railway companies and twenty-eight cities issued foreign bonds. Of the cities, Moscow was the most prolific, with at least forty-three different issues, although many were replacements for earlier loans. Of the State issues, that of 1906 was the largest, with almost £86 million outstanding in 1917. Needless to say, the number of bonds issued, in denominations ranging from £20 (or its equivalent) to £1,000, is quite enormous, but even so individual issues can often be quite small, such as the 1912 City of Nicolaiev 2nd issue which amounted to only £41,620 in total.

The largest holdings of Tsarist bonds were in France and Germany, but following their default and the subsequent World Wars a great many were lost or destroyed. Certainly many of the internal issues (those denominated in

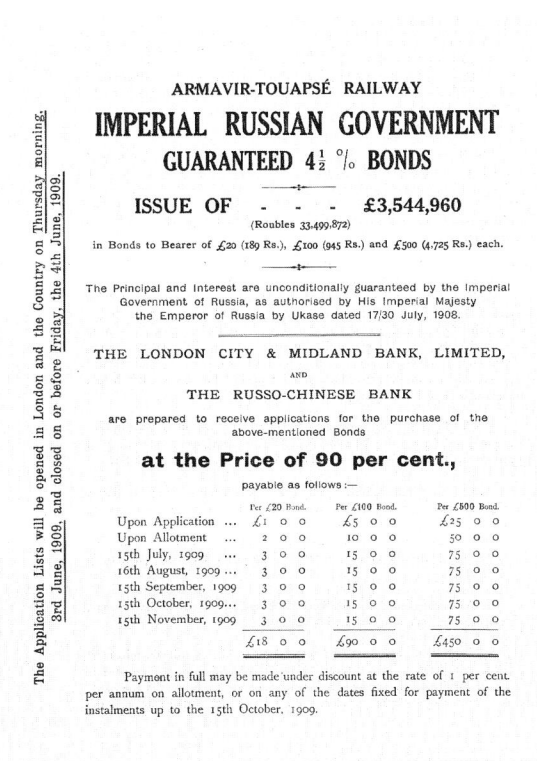

Promotional leaflet for the Armavir-Touapse Railway bond issue of 1909. Related material such as this adds considerable interest to a collection.

65

The Grand Russian Railway Company was established in 1857 and controlled several lines including the St. Petersburg to Warsaw (670 miles). This certificate represents 5 bonds of 125 Roubles each.

Roubles for domestic sale) were destroyed in Russia itself. One might be forgiven for wondering why so many foreigners invested as heavily as they did in Russia. The reasons were simple; higher financial returns (or the promise of them) and the close links which existed between the Russian and European nobility.

As with so many countries it was the growth of railways which resulted in the greatest variation of bonds for the collector.

THE RAILWAYS

Construction lagged behind Europe and America and it was only thanks to the enthusiasm and determination of Tsar Nicolas I that any progress was made at all. The first line, it is true, had little strategic or functional benefit, but it did at least provide a link from St. Petersburg to the summer palace at Tsarskoye-Selo, now known as Pushkin and the birthplace of Alexander II. The line was opened in 1837 but it was not until the following year that steam traction was exclusively used. At that time it was also extended to Pavlovsk — an entertainment resort holding concerts by such notables as Johann Strauss who was resident band-leader in 1860.

The next two lines to be approved for building were the Warsaw-Vienna Railway and the St. Petersburg-Moscow Railway, which was subsequently sold to the Grand Russian Railway Company. These lines were of a more practical nature than Tsarskoye-Selo. Indeed, the Warsaw-Vienna line, which was finished in 1848, was immediately used to transport troops to quell the Hungarian uprising.

Financial skulduggery

The government was unable to agree a single course of action in dealing with the building and financing of the railways. The net effect was of considerable benefit to the entrepreneurial constructors as the government invariably ended up bearing most of the financial risk.

Eventually the construction of the lines was taken on directly by the government, with the intention of selling them, when completed, to private concerns. The proceeds, invested in the government's new 'Railway Fund', were intended to finance the construction of further new lines.

The Railway Fund was initially financed by selling Alaska to the USA and then by selling shares of the various existing railway lines owned by the government. These included the Kursk-Kiev and Nicolas Railways. To supplement the income from the sale of lines, Consolidated bond issues were raised by the government in Europe from 1870 to 1884. The effect of replacing the growing number of individual bond issues with the Consolidated loans helped restore foreign confidence in the Russian economy.

But the drain on the Fund of constructing all these new lines was such that, by 1880, the government only owned about thirty-five miles of operative railway line in the whole of the country. The only thing the government had to show for its denationalization programme was eighty per cent of the railway companies' debt.

CITY LOANS

The number of Russian cities and the quantity of bonds issued by them is appreciably lower than those of the railways and the State and because of this they make an interesting collecting theme which is both achievable and satisfying.

Many issues were extremely small; mention having already been made of the city of Nicolaiev 2nd issue of which there were only fourteen £500 bonds were issued.

Between the period 1891-1915 twenty eight Russian cities raised loans, some, such as Moscow, had several issues so that the total number of City loans exceeded one hundred. On the basis of an average three denominations per issue, this presents the collector with a target of around 300 pieces; not a large figure in itself, but nevertheless a very difficult one to achieve for two main reasons. Firstly, some issues were extremely small, and secondly, several bonds were only issued internally, that is to say they were generally not available outside Russia and were largely destroyed.

The purpose of the loan is often indicated on the back of the bonds themselves and can make interesting reading. The 1912 City of Nicolaiev issues, for example, were issued, among other things, for the 'purchase of the enterprise of the Belgian Company Ltd of the existing tramways of Nicolaiev with horse traction', and perhaps more intriguingly 'for increasing the floating means of the municipal pawnbrokery'!

Most of the foreign-issued bonds bear facsimile signatures of the mayor, two members of the municipal authority and the book-keeper; the latter signature is usually original, as he no doubt had to carry the can if things went wrong. These bonds were quoted on most of the major European stock exchanges (Paris, Berlin, London, Amsterdam and Brussels) and are often written in four languages and denominated in at least three currencies, exchange rates being fixed at that time.

Many of the original Russian city names have changed over the years and it can be an interesting task locating them on a map. In view of the fairly small populations at the turn of the century it is a little difficult to understand what happened to all the money raised. In 1897, for example, the population of Moscow was less than 1 million.

Apart from the economic aspects of the bonds, the designs are also appealing. They rarely carry views of the city (Kharkov being an exception) but invariably portray the municipal crest. In the case of Moscow, for example, this was St. George slaying the dragon.

As with all pre-revolutionary Russian City issues, this £20 bond of the City of Moscow bears the crest of the city, St George slaying the dragon.

Of the old countries to emerge from the the East Bloc and to regain their independence, those of the Baltic States offer the collector an interesting piece of history concerning their bonds.

THE BALTIC STATES

Following the devastation of the First World War, the independent states of Estonia, Latvia and Lithuania proceeded to rebuild their ruined economies. The populace collected gold and other assets to the value of £5.7 million and deposited these with the Bank of England for safe keeping.

By 1940 all three States had been annexed by Russia, which then proceeded to dispose of, or disperse, most of the population. Germany occupied the territories a year later, at which point Britain impounded the Baltic assets by invoking the 'Trading with the Enemy' Act. With the final expulsion

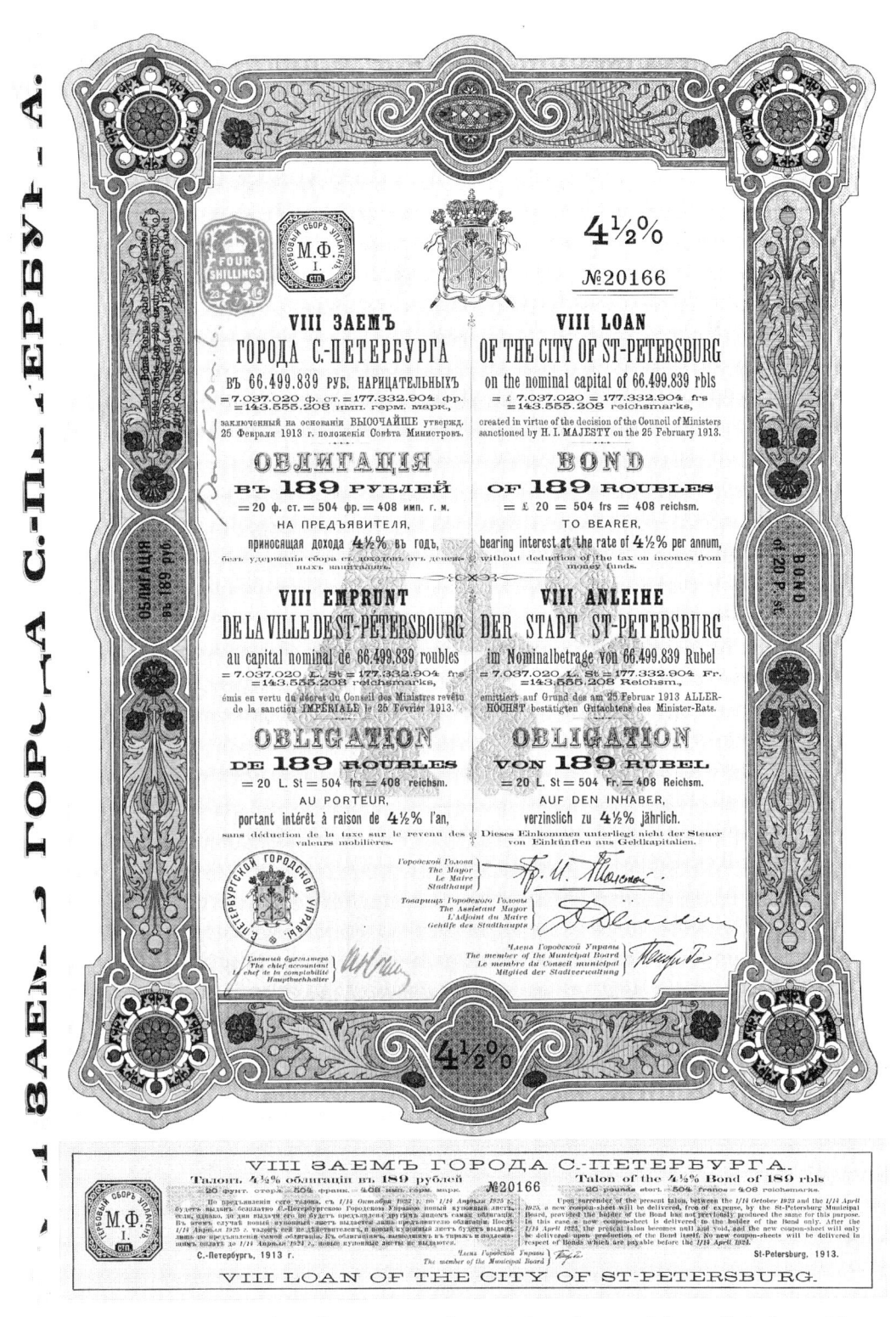

Bonds of the City of St Petersberg (later Leningrad, now St Petersberg again) are all similar to this 1913 issue. Note the French style wavy border on the left and the City's crest top centre.

Engraved by Bradbury Wilkinson, Republic of Estonia bonds were mostly redeemed in the 1969 settlement. Approximately half the total issue is believed to be still outstanding. Vignette of the port and capital, Talinn, as seen from the sea.

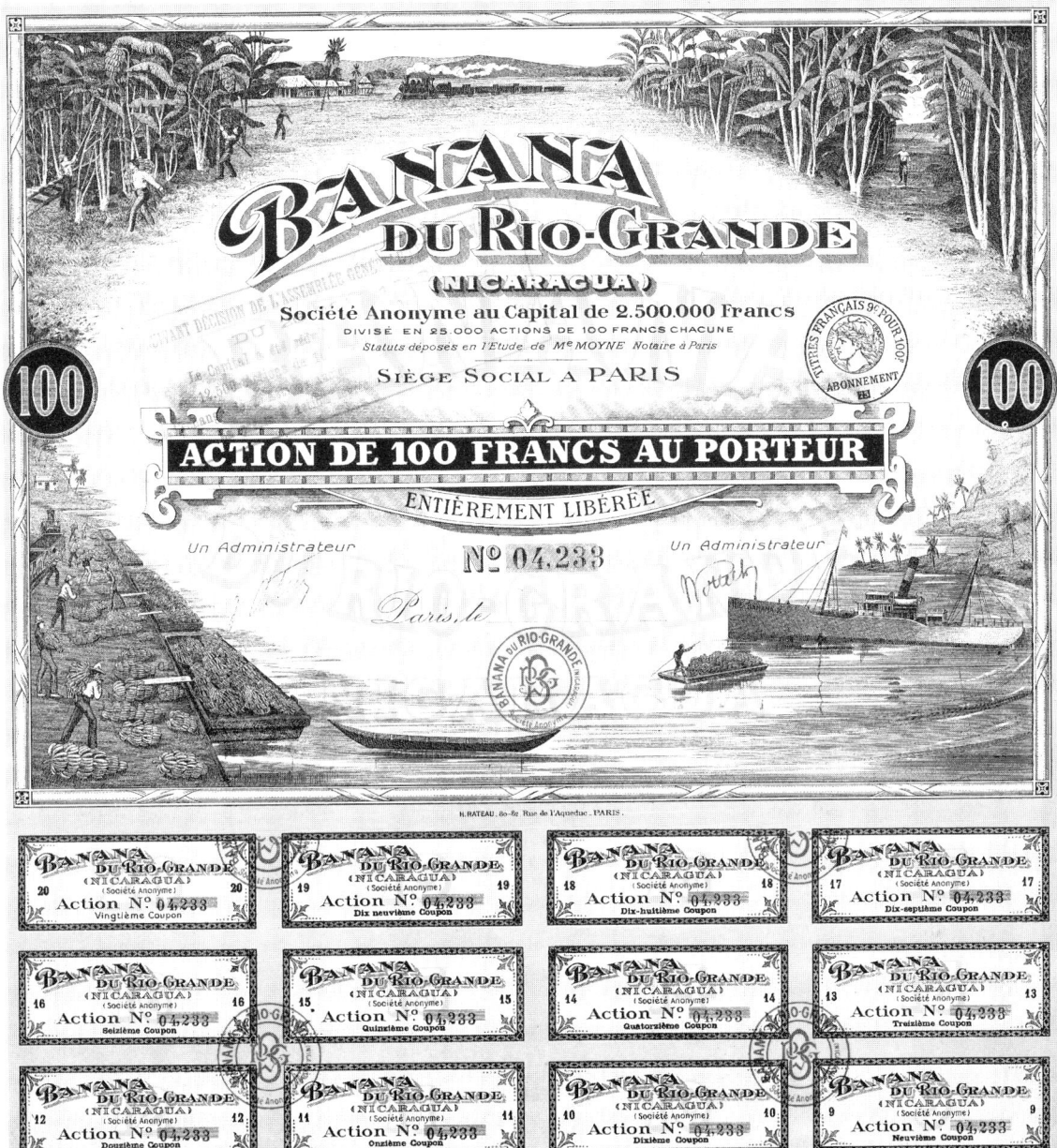

For anyone with a passion for bananas this is a must! Not only is the share in banana yellow, but it also depicts large amounts of the fruit being loaded on the dockside ready for the "Banana X", a ship which would look more at home on an "African Queen" film set.

A rare (only 300 issued), attractive and historically interesting debenture of the Meteor Diamond Mining Company made out to a member of the Mosenthal family. Harry Mosenthal was an original director of De Beers.

The Gunder Syndicate Ltd. One of many small mining companies registered in Kimberley, Cape of Good Hope.

of Germany from Eastern Europe, Russia once more seized the three countries and demanded the return of the Baltic assets.

As a counterclaim Britain sought compensation for owners of bonds issued and defaulted by the Baltic States. The result, in 1969, was a settlement whereby of the £5.7 million of gold £500,000 was used to buy consumer goods for sending to the USSR and the balance was paid out to British holders of the bonds — a story described at the time as 'squalid'. The bonds redeemed in this way included the Republic of Estonia 1927 issue and the Cities of Vilna and Riga.

It is estimated that about 50% of these bonds were settled in 1969.

The story does not stop there. Following independence, Estonia obtained agreement from the British Government that the confiscated assets should not have been used as they were in 1969 and the funds would therefore be refunded.

Russia, in all its guises, offers the serious collector a wealth of material. The settlements have significantly depleted the quantity of bonds available but nevertheless, there is no shortage of interesting and historically fascinating subject matter. Catalogues on Russian Railways and Cities have already been published and other, more detailed, reference books are expected.

SOUTH AFRICA

The commercial history of South Africa since the 1860s has revolved around mineral resources, particularly gold and diamonds and the share certificates issued to finance development of these minerals clearly reflect the excitement and volatility of such a commodity based economy.

The first company to be formed and registered in South Africa in 1800 was the "African Theatre" which initially passed its profits to charity. Despite the establishment of the Cape Town Commercial Exchange in 1817, it was not until the 1830s that commercial activity began in earnest. The first bank was formed in 1831 (Cape of Good Hope Savings Bank) and a variety of other companies sprang up around that period. By this time Britain had taken over the Colony which had resulted in the freeing of all slaves. These were valued at £3 million but a fifty per cent compensation paid by Britain to owners was viewed as inadequate and a major contributory reason for the 'Great Trek' with Boers marching north to found the new lands of the Orange Free State and the Transvaal.

Although the compensation was considered as too small, it did represent a substantial injection of money into the economy thus encouraging business which was further spurred on by the discovery of copper in the 1850s. Reserves, however, were inadequate and the boom soon collapsed. This pattern of boom and crash was to be followed many times in the future.

As the copper trend waned many new companies were formed, particularly following the passing of the Joint Stock Companies Limited Liability Act in 1861. The largest company was the Cape Town Railway & Dock Co., capitalized at £600,000 and the builder of the original railway line to Wellington.

Simmer & Jack Mines. One of the more well known gold mines of the Transvaal. Still in operation but now part of a larger group.

Commercial progress was not limited to Cape Colony and indeed the first railway in South Africa was the Natal Railway Co. which was opened in 1860 and ran between Durban and the Point. The Orange Free State developed rather more slowly, with the most significant company being the Bloemfontein Bank, which was later absorbed by the National Bank of the Orange Free State.

Of all the areas to benefit most from mineral discoveries, the Transvaal was, of course, the greatest.

DIAMONDS AND GOLD

The early diamond exploration companies were little more than syndicates of individuals, but by 1869 more formal organizations were materializing. Of these, the Perserverance Co. and the Spes Bona Co. are perhaps the better known. The earliest flotation was of the Hope Town Diamond Co., later taken

The Oroya Railway connected the coal mines of the Peruvian Andes with the ocean at Callao. The trains ran on petrol rather than coal due to its abundance in the region. This £100 bearer share was issued in Lima in 1878.

over by the London and South Africa Exploration Co. (1870). This latter company acquired the Bullfontein and Dorstfontein areas adjoining Kimberley and was in turn acquired by De Beers in 1899. De Beers itself was formed in 1871.

Fearing that the Zulus were about to overrun the Boer states in 1877, the British annexed Transvaal and eventually beat the Zulus two years later. Unfortunately Britain was slow to hand back the republics, so prompting Paul Kruger to lead a successful rebellion in 1880 reasserting the independence of the Boer territories. This date coincided with the formation of Kimberley's first stock exchange (the second followed one year later) and the great diamond boom had begun in earnest.

Numerous companies (and stock exchanges!) were formed with the total nominal capital invested rising from £2.5 million to £8 million within six months. Seventy one companies were formed, of which thirteen belonged to De Beers. But, as with copper, the boom was short-lived and by mid-1881 the crash had set in, culminating in the auctioning off of one of the stock exchanges. By 1888 most diamond companies had been amalgamated into De Beers.

After the first diamond crash, it was not until 1885 that a major recovery began, this time initiated by the completion of a railway line to the diamond fields, but more significantly influenced by the discovery of gold at Witwatersrand in 1886.

Early gold deposits were so deeply entrenched that mining was difficult and costly. It was primarily the English who could afford it, particularly those, such as Cecil Rhodes, who had already built up

The Cleveland, Cincinnatti, Chicago & St Louis Railway. Incorporated in 1889 as an amalgamation of several lines the company steadily acquired many others, becoming a part of Penn Central in 1938. Classic vignette of cowboy crossing river, which appears on several stocks and bonds.

their fortunes from diamond mining.

Again several local stock exchanges were set up and in 1889 South Africa had more stockbroking firms per head of population than anywhere else in the world, 750 broking firms served a total (white) population of only half a million. During the gold boom years of 1888-9, the newspapers published editions every hour but, as before, the crash came. This time it was relatively short-lived and the formation of Rand Mines Ltd. in 1893 was a sign of renewed stability.

THE BOER WAR AND AFTER

War was declared on Britain in 1899 and following many prolonged and bloody encounters was lost by 1902. But it was not until 1910 that the various states of the Transvaal, Orange Free State, Cape Colony and Natal amalgamated to form the Union of South Africa under the premiership of Louis Botha.

The Johannesburg Stock Exchange was inaugurated in 1904 and in 1917 Ernest Oppenheimer formed the Anglo American Corporation of South Africa. At the time of the Union there were 7,570 miles of railway track in the country, mostly state owned, but composed of three quite different systems: The Central South African Railways, The Cape Government Railways, and The Natal Government Railways. It was not until 1916 that agreement could be reached on a merger.

The history of South Africa is closely interwoven with the discovery of precious minerals and their commercial development. The share certificates of the period reflect this process extremely well and provide a compact theme for anyone seeking a link with mining industries. Added interest comes from some of the signatures of those early "prospectors" and some, such as Barney Barnato, Alfred Beit and Joseph B Robinson can significantly affect value.

CENTRAL & SOUTH AMERICA

Representing one-sixth of the world's land mass, South America has always offered, since its invasion by the Spanish and Portuguese, more hope and excitement to investors than any other part of the world. Containing only one-twentieth of the world's population and enormous mineral reserves ranging from gold to oil, the continent is only now beginning to properly develop its resources.

Until Napoleon's defeat of Spain, the continent was totally dominated by its colonisers and seen as little more than a source of wealth to be plundered and taken back to Europe (pirates willing). Following a period of uncertainty it was not long before the countries began to establish their independence. This was generally encouraged by Britain and by 1822, the new states were actively seeking finance from the European markets. At the time, London was short of investment opportunities in country debt and despite some suspect fundraising by early emissaries of those countries, the first major "official" loan to Colombia, was well received. Success of the Colombian Loan encouraged

The Buenos Ayres Tramways Company owned concessions for the running of a number of lines in Buenos Ayres, the majority under electric traction. A portrait of the Chairman, Dr. Teofilo Lacroze appears on the debentures which are signed by the London director, Miguel Lacroze. The company's assets were nationalised without compensation.

others to follow. Thoughts of untapped wealth did much to outweigh professional caution and it was in this market that Gregor Macgregor (see page 113) was able to launch his totally fraudulent bonds of the "Kingdom of Poyais". Not perhaps surprisingly, those early (genuine) loans soon failed giving Colombia the doubtful honour of being the first country to default on a major sterling debt, closely followed by Argentina, who in 1843 thoughtfully offered up the Falkland Islands as settlement — the Government pointed out that they were already British territory.

International recognition of the new world countries was slow, particularly by Spain and Portugal (not too surprising really). Brazil, for example, was not recognized by Portugal as an independent nation until 1825, becoming a republic in 1899. One of the first prosperous industries to develop in Brazil was that of sugar cane, but gold and diamonds from the area of Minas Gerais were the big crowd pullers, resulting in the growth of Rio de Janeiro as a major port. In the nineteenth century commodities such as rubber and coffee became principally important and these were supplemented by large reserves of iron ore.

The difficult terrain of the continent made inland development difficult and most of the railways tend to be short lines linking up with the coastal ports. Only three major areas of extensive railway networks exist; these are the Argentinian Pampas, South Eastern Brazil and Central Chile. The railways were of course built and financed by foreigners, and the various share certificates and bonds issued at the time represent a major collecting segment in this sector. The bonds and debentures, in particular, are extremely attractive, often engraved by Waterlow, as in the case of the Brazil Railway Co., which became the holding company of many of the country's railways. Many of the original locomotives remain in service, several of which are still wood burners.

Apart from railways, the South American enthusiast is presented with a wide variety of material, including banks, mines and State loans. Over recent years many Government bonds have been redeemed after falling into default, thus reducing the number of outstanding certificates available for collectors. Not all have yet undergone a repayment programme, however, and there are always those around keen to speculate on Mexican and Cuban paper.

Central and South American material for many reasons is highly collectable. It is attractive, relatively scarce and has an 'international flavour' such as that of China and Russia. Much research still needs to be done on the area but with subjects ranging from Macgregor's Poyais, the Panama Canal (see page 135) and construction of the foreign-owned railways, the scripophilist has a fascinating opportunity to acquire a most interesting and attractive cross section.

UNITED STATES OF AMERICA

American material is so rich in history and art that some background to the economic development of the country is essential. With the exception of the landing of the Mayflower and the eventual Declaration of Independence in 1776 three major events were primarily responsible for shaping the commercial development of the United States, prior to the twentieth century. The first of these was the building of the railroads which began in 1830 and continued for the following seventy years; the second was the discovery and exploitation of minerals, possibly most glamorously portrayed by the California Gold Rush of 1849; and the third was the Civil War of 1861-5. These three features are most amply depicted by the bond and share issues of the time.

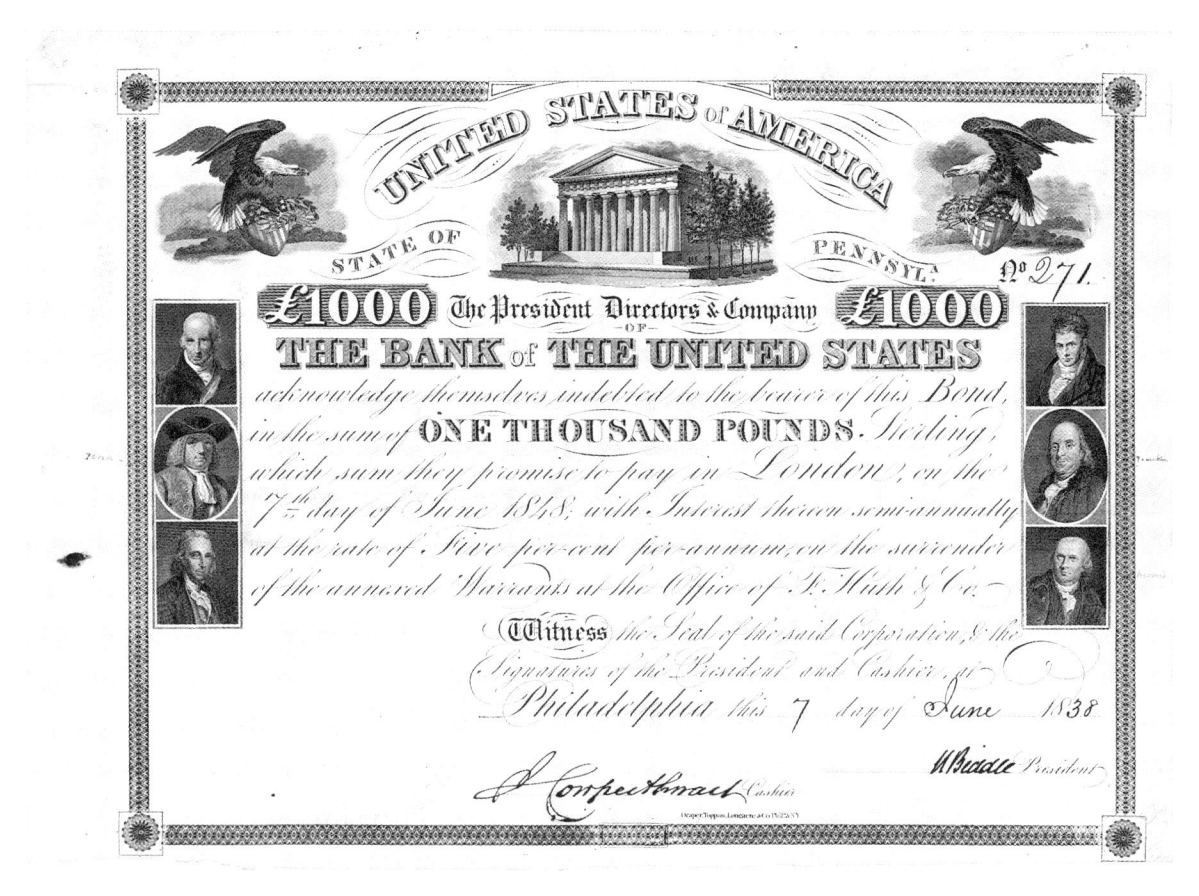

Rare bond issued by the Second Bank of the United States signed by Biddle as President and depicting 6 famous Americans; Rittenhouse (Director of the Mint), Penn (founder of Pennsylvania) and Paine (author of the "Rights of Man") on the left from top and Robert Fulton, Benjamin Franklin and Robert Morris on the right.

EARLY COMMERCIAL & BANKING ACTIVITY

So far as the scripophilist is concerned the earliest and easiest date around which to find American share certificates is 1795. The New York Stock Exchange was formally inaugurated by the "Buttonwood Agreement" of 1792 and there was little earlier corporate activity other than by companies formed and operated by Britain. This is not to say that no shares exist prior to this date, merely that they are rare and difficult to obtain. Interesting examples are those of two companies formed by Benjamin Franklin; the "Library Company of Philadelphia" (1789) and the even earlier "Pennsylvania Hospital", America's first incorporated hospital formed in 1751. The two certificates most frequently seen are those of the "North American Land Company" (signed by Robert Morris) and the "Philadelphia & Lancaster Turnpike" (often signed by William Bingham), both signatories played key roles in the financial development of the United States and it is interesting to follow the interlinked activities of these and one other of the more powerful Philadelphis families, that of Nicholas Biddle.

Fine example of a share in the Philadelphia & Lancaster Turnpike signed by William Bingham and dated 1795. Printed on vellum this is the earliest known American item with a vignette.

Robert Morris

Born in England, Morris joined his father's tobacco exporting business in Maryland in 1746 and later the well known Philadelphia shipping business, "Willings", later "Willing, Morris & Co." where he became a highly successful businessman and politician. His official postings allowed him to not only benefit the Government but also to substantially increase his personal fortune. As a close friend of George Washington and signatory of the Declaration of Independence, Morris was persuaded to accept the appointment of Superintendent of Finance which in turn provided him with the opportunity of establishing the Bank of North America and making further personal profit. Land speculation proved to be his final downfall with the North American Land Company as one of his prime vehicles. At one time Morris and a partner owned most of the land on which Washington DC is built today.

Disaster struck in 1798 when he was arrested by his creditors and sent to debtor's prison, where Washington visited him. He was released after three years and died penniless in 1806.

Marietta & North Georgia Railway Company. $1000 bond payable "in gold coin of the United States in the City of Boston".

Fine looking bond issued in 1848 for the City of Boston. Signed by Josiah Quincy, one time Mayor of Boston and President of Harvard for 16 years.

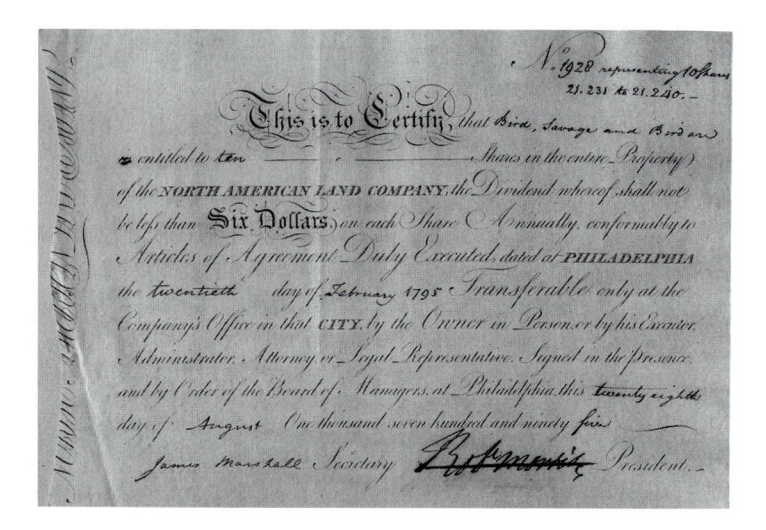

The North American Land Company. Classic early American share signed by Robert Morris as President. A signatory of the Declaration of Independence, Morris was a friend of George Washington and a founder of the Bank of North America.

William Bingham

Born in Philadelphia, Bingham married the daughter of Thomas Willing (of "Willings", the same company with which Robert Morris made his name) and became a founder and director of the Pennsylvania Bank later renamed the "Bank of North America", the country's first chartered bank formed as a direct result of the activities of Robert Morris. He became a major land owner and powerful financier. Both his daughters married into the Baring family with whom he worked closely at one time, selling them one million acres of Maine for 33 cents an acre.

Bingham was president of the "Philadelphia & Lancaster Turnpike Road", the first of its kind in the United States. It was 62 miles long and cost $465,000 to build. The share certificates are the first to carry a vignette and are finely engraved on vellum. Bingham signed many of the shares which still exist today, several of which carry a series of endorsements on the back indicating their progressive ownership. It is interesting to note that many passed through the Biddle family — another link in the chain of influential Philadelphia financiers.

Alexander Hamilton

Perhaps of all those involved in the formulation and development of early America following the War of Independence, Alexander Hamilton was the most influential. Born in the West Indies and showing early promise, Hamilton was sent to America by his friends and relatives for schooling. He became closely aligned with the colonial cause and in the course of fighting for the Revolution, was introduced to George Washington becoming his private secretary in 1777.

After studying law, Washington appointed him first Secretary of the Treasury with the task of settling War Debts and reorganising public finances. Hamilton was a controversial and aggressive operator who went about his task with enthusiasm. He proposed and had Congress incorporate the country's first National Bank (the "Bank of the United States") in 1791 despite considerable opposition. Even after leaving public life he continued to philosophise and comment on economic progress, establishing himself as the "patron saint of capitalism, nationalism and aristocratic traditions in America".

His controversial and determined style eventually resulted in his death following a duel with an arch rival, Aaron Burr, leader of the Democratic party in New York.

Nicholas Biddle & the Second Bank of the United States

In the period between the demise of the "First Bank of the United States" and creation of the "Second" in 1816, The country suffered a total breakdown of the banking and currency system, a situation greatly exacerbated by the War with Great Britain in 1812. The "Second Bank of the United States" was formed to stop the rot but in its early years it was run more as a commercial enterprise than a government body, not particularly surprising perhaps as the Government only owned one fifth of its capital. However, its involvement in property based lending resulted in some serious political upsets. In particular, the Bank upset Andrew Jackson.

After a spell of consolidation Nicholas Biddle was appointed President in 1822. A capable but tempestuous person, he soon re-established the Bank on its course as a true "Central Bank". Biddle did much to strengthen credibility overseas by working closely with Barings in London and Hope in Amsterdam. A large amount of the Bank's stock was sold to European investors and many of the share certificates which turn up today (usually signed by Biddle) originated in England. Despite his efforts, Biddle eventually lost the battle with Jackson and in 1836 the Bank began to wind down. After a brief spell as "Bank of the United States of Pennsylvania" it finally closed its doors in 1841.

Apart from the well known shares of the Philadelphia & Lancaster Turnpike, North American Land Company and Benjamin Franklin's commercial enterprises, the period prior to 1800 is one which has been much neglected by collectors. This is gradually changing. Early turnpike shares and bonds issued to finance the Revolutionary War are not difficult to find and the latter, at least, are well documented (see Anderson's "The Price of Liberty"). This is an exciting period in American history and offers the scripophilist great opportunities.

IMPROVED COMMUNICATIONS

The first steam railway, the Baltimore and Ohio, was opened in 1830. Early development of the railroads is covered in some detail in the later chapter on 'Railways' and further background is provided by the story of Vanderbilt in the chapter on 'Signatures'. Both the railway certificates themselves and their often famous signatories each make fascinating collecting themes.

One of the most appealing features of these certificates is their visual excitement. Most are engraved on good quality paper and carry vignettes of locomotives or related scenes. The bonds are usually of specific issue as stated on the document itself, although some issues were dependent on the number of miles of track actually built. Many, such as that of the Blue Ridge Railroad Co., were guaranteed by the State in gold, while others were issued by a state on behalf of a railroad company, such as the $1,000 bonds of 1868 issued by North Carolina to finance the Wilmington Charlotte and Rutherford Railroad Co.

Material from Hawaii is scarce, as is this share of the Hawaiian Bell Telephone Company.

There were reputed to be over 9,000 different US railroad companies formed over the seventy years or so of railway expansion. Many progressed no further than printing their share certificates, but many others prospered and attracted the attention of most of the financial wizards of the time.

The prospective collector of US railway certificates is faced with a wide range of prices and specialist sub-fields. Modern certificates (around 1940) with train vignettes can be picked up at little cost, whereas early material, particularly pre-1850, can be expensive, particularly if signed by one of the "Railroad Barons". The collector with an eye to investment is recommended to select pieces bearing famous signatures, and/or early dates.

GOLD!

In May 1848 while railroads were expanding and edging out towards the west, the California gold rush began. The same year the State was ceded to the United States following the Mexican War.

The impact on the development of the West Coast was enormous. The population grew from 26,000 in 1848 to 115,000 by the end of 1849. About a quarter of the increase was due to immigrants from Europe, Australia and China and many formed themselves into small companies. There are many interesting companies of the period, often with low capital and consequently small share issues, and the sector makes an interesting collecting field both as a part of the overall framework of the United States and as a separate subject which can easily be expanded to encompass other gold discoveries of the time such as those in Australia and South Africa.

But it was not only gold and other precious metals which were discovered. Coal, copper and iron ore were equally important, albeit not so glamorous. Many certificates, this time from the East Coast, bear witness to these developments.

THE CIVIL WAR

In an earlier chapter attention was drawn to the historical significance of Confederate Bonds issued to finance the Civil War of 1861-65. Here attention is concentrated on the intrinsic nature of the bonds themselves — how they were printed, how many were issued and where they are now.

Lack of funds and time meant that little attention was paid to the quality of printing of both banknotes and bonds issued by the Confederacy. As a result, counterfeiting was prevalent, but it would appear that this was concentrated on the banknote side rather than the bonds, which were a little better controlled. The poor quality of paper used, however, has resulted in the gradual disintegration of a great many certificates over the years. As many as ten different companies were used to print the bonds.

The number of bonds issued has been determined by reference to the original Acts of Congress and the results have been catalogued (see bibliography). There are approximately 170 different bond types and a further ninety or so variations. Thus it is feasible to complete a collection, but certainly not easy, due to the relatively small issues of certain bonds (several, less than 500). Although the

Many Confederate bonds depict the government officials. This bond portrays General "Stonewall" Jackson, one of the South's great heroes from the Battle of Bull Run.

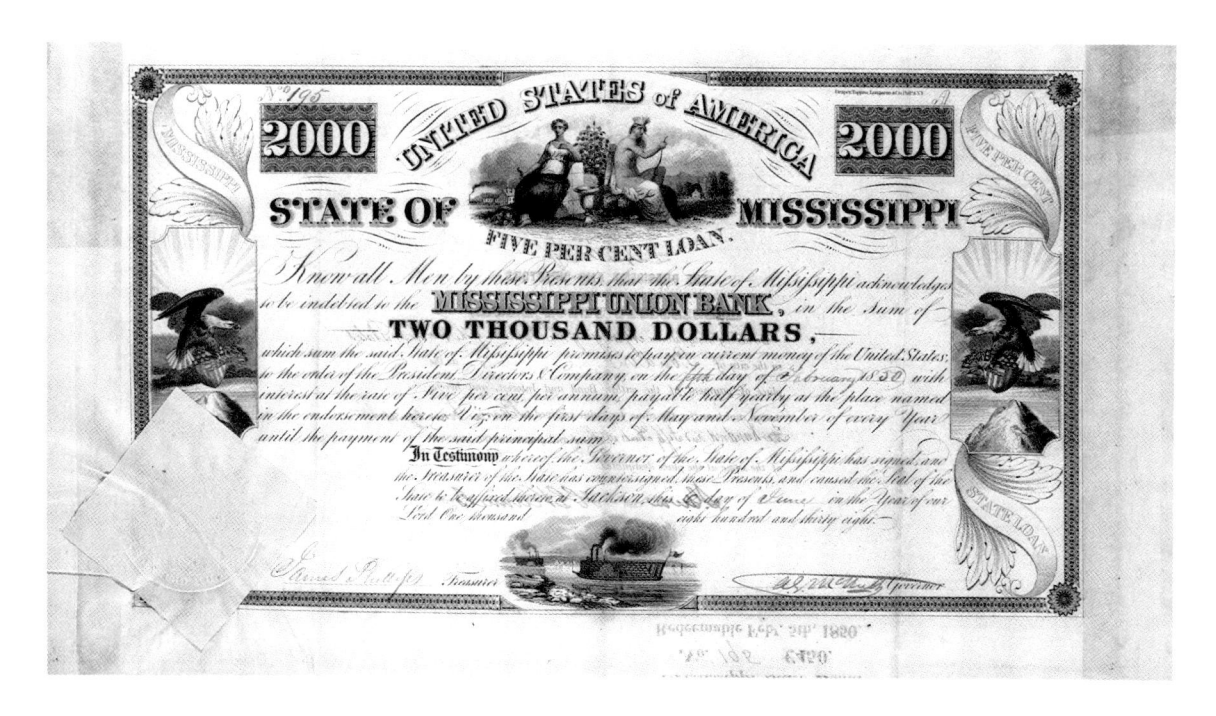

The 1838 Union Bank issue of the State of Mississippi. Still in default!

amount of money raised in total by the Confederates was vast, this is not quite the same as saying that the number of pieces of paper was equally vast. Most of the bonds are high denominations, $500 or $1,000 or more, thus considerably limiting the quantities issued.

To answer the question of where they are now we must remember that the vast majority of the bonds were sold in Europe, particularly Britain and France, to those keen to maintain a steady flow of cotton for the flourishing mills of the period. With the loss of the war and the consequent default, a council was established in England with the objective of recovering all or some of the debt. Bondholders were invited to place their bonds with the council in return for 'scrip certificates' proving ownership and indicating that the bonds were being held by the National Safe Deposit Company Limited. Over the years the deposited bonds were moved on several occasions eventually ending up in the vaults of Coutts Bank in London. After much consideration the holding (comprising 75,000 bonds) was eventually sold at auction in 1987 and the bonds dispersed across the globe.

THE MISSISSIPPI BONDS

One particularly interesting group of bonds which pre-dated Confederate material and is still in default are those issued under the guarantee of the State of Mississippi in the 1830s.

There are two types, those issued by the Planters Bank in denominations of $1000, and those issued by the Union Bank in denominations of $2000. They were issued as follows:
- $500,000 (500 bonds) by the Planters Bank in 1831
- $1,500,000 (1500 bonds) by the Planters Bank in 1833
- $5,000,000 (2500 bonds) by the Union Bank in 1838

Most were bought in Europe with the Union Bank bonds being actively sold by Nicholas Biddle. Interest was paid for some years but in 1841 both issues fell into default causing considerable

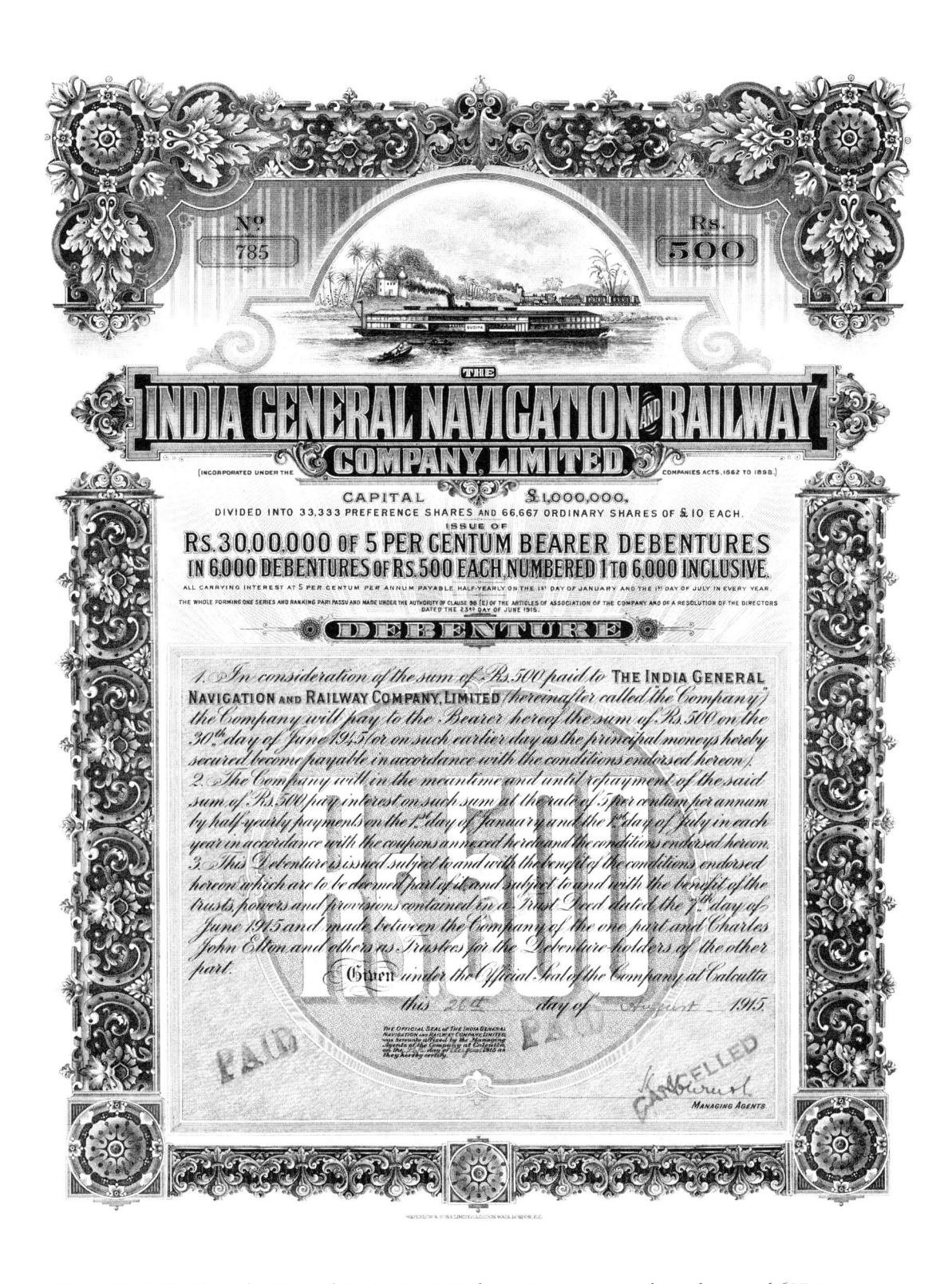

Formed in 1899, the India General Navigation & Railway Company owned a railway and 627 river vessels, some of which still operate on the inland waterways of Bengal and Assam.

political and financial upset. Several legal battles were fought culminating in the Supreme Court of Mississippi declaring the repudiation as improper. A later action was brought under the banner of the Principality of Monaco, but again without success. No doubt someone somewhere will always consider a settlement chase worthwhile.

Out of a total of 2000 bonds issued by the Planters Bank, 88 were redeemed in exchange for land rights and 464 were donated by the philanthropist George Peabody to the "Southern Education Fund" (later, Mississippi University).

OTHER COUNTRIES

Inevitably space constraints make it impossible to adequately describe the material of all countries in the world. Many of those omitted from this section are referred to in others under various themes. Lack of more detailed comment on such countries as Spain, Italy, Greece, India and Scandinavia does not imply a dearth of material from those countries and hopefully many of the bonds illustrated will dispel that view.

We now turn to themes by subject. Subjects can be defined by a time period or more usually by an activity such as mining or banking.

Collecting Themes by Subject

EARLY MATERIAL

It is not easy to find material 200-300 years old for obvious reasons, nevertheless items are available and many such pieces are full of historical significance. A few examples are given here.

The Spanish Trading Companies

Formed under Royal patronage, the Spanish trading companies were created to match the dominant activities of the Dutch and British India Companies. They were established during the 18th Century and each was granted a specific monopoly either by product or, more usually, geographic area of trading, thus giving them a significant advantage over other potential companies.

They can be divided into two groups; those concerned with overseas trade and those which operated internally.

Examples from the first group were:
- Companhia de Honduras (1714)
- Companhia de Caracas (1728), one of the most profitable which eventually "merged" into the Companhia de Filipinas.
- Companhia de Habana (1740) which controlled the trade between Spain and Cuba.
- Companhia de Barcelona (1755). Held the monopoly of trade with Santo Domingo, Puerto Rico and Margarita, none of which locations proved particularly profitable.
- Companhia de Filipinas (1785). The most profitable of all the companies controlling trade with the American colonies. It failed following the outbreak of war between Spain and England in 1796.

Shares in the early Spanish trading companies are magnificent. This share in the Companhia de Barcelona dated 1758 depicts the City and the Virgin of Montserrat together with the arms of Spain and Catalonia. The certificate is printed on vellum.

Examples of the internal companies which were mainly concerned with the Spanish textile industry are:
- Companhia de Zarza la Mayor (1746)
- Real Companhia de Commercio y Fabricas de Zaragoza
- Real Companhia de San Fernando de Sevilla (1747)

Share certificates of the Spanish Trading companies are some of the most elaborate in the world with large format designs incorporating religious and geographic images. Most are printed on vellum and tend to fetch high prices at auction (about $3000-$6000).

The Bank of England

Needing money for the French-Dutch War, the British Government passed the Bank of England Act in 1694. The Bank was granted "Rates and Duties upon the Tunnage of Ships and Vessels, and upon Beer, Ale and other Liquors". Such taxes were to be used by the Bank to pay interest to those individuals who subscribed for the Bank's Stock.

Cons ou   *Sieur Marin Jouffet*

Grosse   *8. mars 1700*

PARDEVANT les Conseillers du Roy, Notaires Gardenottes & Garde-Scels de sa Majesté au Chastelet de Paris, soussignez. FURENT presens CLAUDE BOSC Chevalier, Seigneur d'Yvry-sur-Seine, & autres lieux, Conseiller du Roy en ses Conseils, Procureur General de la Cour des Aydes, Prevost des Marchands, Nobles hommes François Regnault Conseiller du Roy, l'un des Quarteniers de cette Ville; François Jean Dionis aussi Conseiller du Roy, Notaire audit Chastelet; Leonard Chauvin Conseiller du Roy en l'Hostel de Ville, & Jean Hallé Marchand bourgeois & ancien Consul, tous Echevins de cette Ville de Paris, LESQUELS en execution du Contract de vente & alienation faite par Messieurs les Commissaires du Conseil, Procureurs speciaux de sa Majesté, en vertu de ses Lettres patentes, ausdits Sieurs Prevost des Marchands & Echevins, de *huit* millions de livres actuels & effectifs de Rente, au Denier vingt, creez par Edit du mois de Decembre 1699. registré où besoin a esté, & pour les causes y contenuës, à les avoir & prendre generalement sur tous les Deniers provenans des Droits des Aydes & Gabelles, que sa Majesté a specialement & par Privilege affectez & hypotequez, au payement & continuation desdits *huit* millions de Rente, & ordonné que les Constitutions en soient faites par lesdits Sieurs Prevost des Marchands & Echevins, à ceux qui voudront les acquerir, pour en joüir par eux, leurs successeurs & ayans cause, pleinement & paisiblement, comme de leur propre chose, vray & loyal acquest, suivant leurs Contracts, & en estre payez par chacun an à Bureau ouvert, en deux payemens égaux de demie année en demie année, actuellement & effectivement, sous leurs simples quittances, par les Receveurs & Payeurs des Rentes, mesme du Quartier d'Octobre, Novembre & Decembre de l'Année derniere 1699. accordé par ledit Edit aux Acquereurs desdites Rentes, en quelque temps dudit Quartier qu'ils en fournissent les principaux au Tresor Royal de Sa Majesté, sans que lesdites Rentes puissent estre retranchées ny reduites pour quelque cause & occasion que ce soit, ny les Acquereurs dépossedez, sinon en les remboursant en un seul & actuel payement des sommes portées par leurs Contracts, & des arrerages qui en seront lors dûs & échûs, frais & loyaux-cousts, le tout en payant actuellement en deniers comptans és mains du Sieur Garde du Tresor Royal, le prix de leurs acquisitions, à raison du Denier vingt, chacun desquels Contracts de Constitutions, sera au moins de cent livres de Rente actuelle par an, avec faculté accordée par sa Majesté, conformément à son Edit du mois de Decembre 1674. aux Estrangers non naturalisez, & ceux demeurans hors du Royaume, Païs, Terres & Seigneuries de son obeïssance de pouvoir acquerir desdites Rentes, ainsi que si c'estoit ses propres Sujets, mesme en disposer entre-vifs, où par Testament, en quelque sorte & maniere que ce puisse estre, Et en cas qu'ils n'en ayent disposé, que leurs heritiers leur succedent, encore que leurs donataires, legataires, ou heritiers, soient Estran-

Mr Legrand

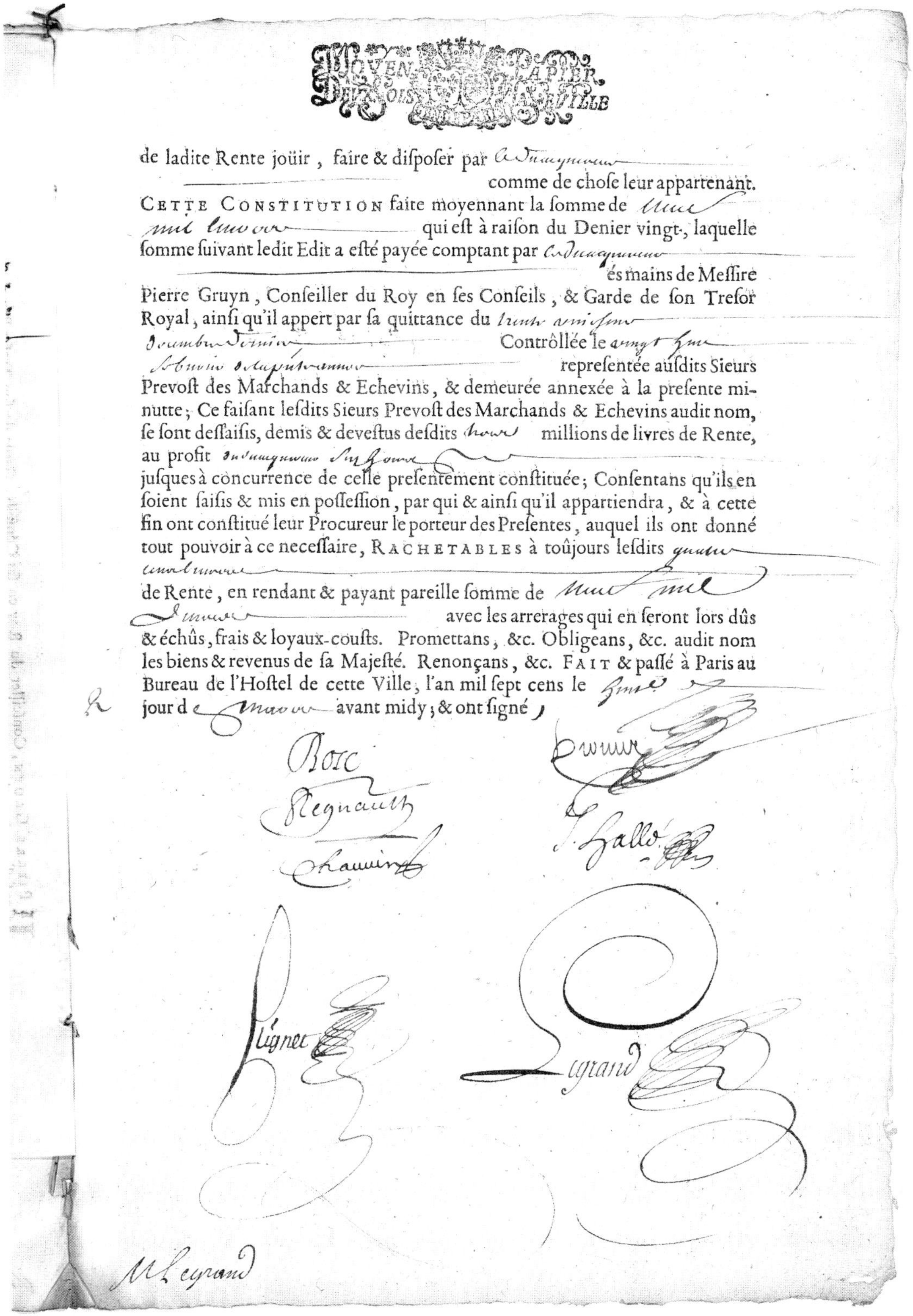

ROYEN PAPIER DEUX SOLS LA FEUILLE

de ladite Rente joüir, faire & disposer par comme de chose leur appartenant. CETTE CONSTITUTION faite moyennant la somme de qui est à raison du Denier vingt, laquelle somme suivant ledit Edit a esté payée comptant par és mains de Messire Pierre Gruyn, Conseiller du Roy en ses Conseils, & Garde de son Tresor Royal, ainsi qu'il appert par sa quittance du Contrôllée le representée ausdits Sieurs Prevost des Marchands & Echevins, & demeurée annexée à la presente minutte; Ce faisant lesdits Sieurs Prevost des Marchands & Echevins audit nom, se sont dessaisis, demis & devestus desdits millions de livres de Rente, au profit jusques à concurrence de celle presentement constituée; Consentans qu'ils en soient saisis & mis en possession, par qui & ainsi qu'il appartiendra, & à cette fin ont constitué leur Procureur le porteur des Presentes, auquel ils ont donné tout pouvoir à ce necessaire, RACHETABLES à toûjours lesdits de Rente, en rendant & payant pareille somme de avec les arrerages qui en seront lors dûs & échûs, frais & loyaux-cousts. Promettans, &c. Obligeans, &c. audit nom les biens & revenus de sa Majesté. Renonçans, &c. FAIT & passé à Paris au Bureau de l'Hostel de cette Ville, l'an mil sept cens le jour d avant midy; & ont signé

Typical French Rente showing the first and third pages of the document. This one was issued in 1700. Note the duty stamp at top of signature page.

Fine example of South Sea Bubble material. When crisis was looming the British Government borrowed money on behalf of the South Sea Company. This Government exchequer bill was issued in 1720 and signed by Lord Halifax.

633 people subscribed raising £1.5 million which was then lent to the Government at 8%. These original subscribers (or shareholders) and subsequent owners held evidence of their investment in the form of an "inscribed stock receipt" rather than a share certificate. The subscribers name was entered in the books of the Bank and any transfer of ownership recorded accordingly.

In 1708 the Bank was granted a virtual monopoly as issuer of banknotes and after a tempestuous period throughout the eighteenth century, during which it was attacked by the Gordan Rioters, it was eventually established as the manager of the National Debt and ultimately nationalised in 1946.

Inscribed Stock Receipts do appear from time to time and make interesting additions to a collection. Prices are very much dependent on age.

The Royal Loans of France

Raising money on the strength of future tax revenues was usual for European governments. From 1522 France began raising large sums by this means, issuing annuities (or "rentes") to those willing to part with a capital sum for the promise of a fixed rate of interest. The rentes were secured on specific taxes and basically took two forms; those issued for the lifetime of the investor, known as "viagère", and those issued with an indefinite life, known as "perpetuelle".

The viagère commanded a higher rate of interest thus encouraging the financiers of the time to have such rentes written in the name of young, healthy children. A variation on this type was the "Tontine" which allowed several parties to be named with the survivors gradually taking larger proportions until eventually the last to die took the lot. Such schemes did much for the murder rate and were eventually banned in 1770 (although the technique was used in Britain many years later).

So far as the collector is concerned French rentes dated prior to 1689 are almost impossible to find but those issued between 1770 and 1789 are more easily available. Louis XIV (the "Sun King") and his successors was frequently in need of money to fight wars, equip lavish palaces and compensate for poor harvests and, after all, there was a limit as to how much could be extracted from the peasants — a limit finally reached in 1789 with the guillotine!

Rentes make an interesting collectable theme and the subject is thoroughly documented in Shakespeare's "The Royal Loans".

Syria Ottoman Railway Company share of 1893. The company was formed to construct a line from Akka to Damascus via Haifa. Despite work being supervised by Sir Douglas and Francis Fox, builders of the Crystal Palace, the line was not completed and was acquired by the Ottoman Government in 1903.

The South Sea "Bubble"

The South Sea Company created by Robert Harley in 1711, was perhaps the most celebrated and earliest of corporate disasters. Formed to trade with Spanish America, investors were persuaded to exchange State Annuities for South Sea stock priced at a hefty premium. The company eventually took over the whole of the National Debt, and its stock, with a guaranteed 6% yield, rocketed from a price of 128.5 in January 1720 to 1000 in July of the same year. Two months later the bubble burst and the price collapsed to 175. Collectors of South Sea material will generally only find inscribed stock receipts as share certificates were not issued. Shareholders were recorded in the company's books and evidence of their holding was provided in the form of receipts — plainly printed but important pieces of financial history.

RAILWAYS

What is it about railways that fascinates so many people? Is it the gleaming brass fittings, the clouds of smoke or the endless lengths of track? All presumably play their part but one thing is certain, of all the inventions since the industrial revolution, none matched the railway for public enthusiasm both at birth and during life.

This book is about bonds and shares, not railways, a subject on which much has already been written, but our paths cross as the building of railways needed financing — a lot of financing, and it is this aspect which concerns the scripophilist.

The Middlesbrough & Guisbrough Railway. Early share, unusually attractive for an English Railway company. Note the cut corner indicating cancellation.

EARLY DAYS

The earliest 'railway' (that is to say, a vehicle drawn by a horse along wooden rails) is believed to have been built in 1603 at Wollaton, England. Many such tracks followed but it was not until around 1780 that wooden rails were replaced by cast iron. By 1810 there were already 300 miles of track in Britain. The development was encouraged by the increasing cost of transport, particularly for minerals — thus most of the lines grew up in the industrial areas, notably the Midlands, the North East and Cornwall.

It was in Cornwall that the idea of steam traction was born. Being the centre of tin mining, stationary steam engines were already in active use, but it was the son of the Dolcoath Mine's manager, Richard Trevithick, who first attempted to introduce the mobile engine. In 1803 he succeeded in driving his steam carriage up the Tottenham Court Road in London, much to the amusement, derision and shock of passers-by. Lack of money and patience caused him to abandon further development work, but others continued, albeit slowly, and over the next twenty years only thirty experimental locomotives were built — all slower than the reliable horse.

The year 1825 saw the opening of the Stockton and Darlington, the first steam-drawn passenger and freight railway in the world. The engine, built by George Stephenson, was named 'Locomotion' and was aided on parts of the track by an occasional horse. The line soon began to make money, with dividends rising from 2.5% in 1826 to 8% in 1832 and to 15% in 1839.

Investors were encouraged, but it was the even greater success of the Liverpool and Manchester Railway which really sparked the 'mania' (the name given to the investment enthusiasm). The directors of the Liverpool and Manchester offered a prize of £500 to the designer of a locomotive which had to be less than six tons, able to pull a load three times its own weight and travel at a minimum speed of 10 mph. The winner was, of course, Stephenson's 'Rocket', with an incredible top speed of 30 mph. The Liverpool and Manchester was the first wholly mechanical railway being worked entirely by steam traction. From the outset it was a fantastic financial success and regularly paid a 9.52% dividend — an appreciably better return than Government securities.

The early British railways were largely financed by the local aristocracy and nouveau riche industrialists. Of the 4,233⅓ shares issued for the Liverpool and Manchester, nearly half were taken up by local citizens and one thousand of the remainder by the Marquess of Stafford. Share certificates of the railway dated 1829-30 are printed on vellum and are one of the earliest railway items available. Those most often seen of the Stockton and Darlington tend to be preference shares issued in 1859, and as such reflect the decline in railway earnings around that period, which led investors to demand the greater security of preference shares and debentures, as opposed to ordinary common stock.

Fairly typical format of a sterling bond issued to finance a Russian Railway. This one was for the Black Sea-Kuban Railway and was issued in 1911.

OVERSEAS DEVELOPMENT

Britain was primarily responsible for the building of many early overseas networks. By 1839 export orders for British locomotives were so large that a shortage of materials developed. As well as locomotives being exported, Welsh coal was specially shipped to stoke the boilers of trains in South America and, more significantly, expertise. Robert Stephenson, for example travelled from Brazil to Russia designing and building the world's great railways. The table below lists the first commercial steam railways in the major industrialised countries:

YEAR	COUNTRY	LINE
1825	Great Britain	Stockton & Darlington
1830	USA	Baltimore & Ohio
1832	France	Paris-St. Germain
1832	Austria	Budweis-Linz
1835	Germany	Nurnberg-Furth
1837	Russia	St. Petersburg-Pavlovsk
1839	Holland	Amsterdam-Haarlem
1844	Switzerland	Zurich-Basle

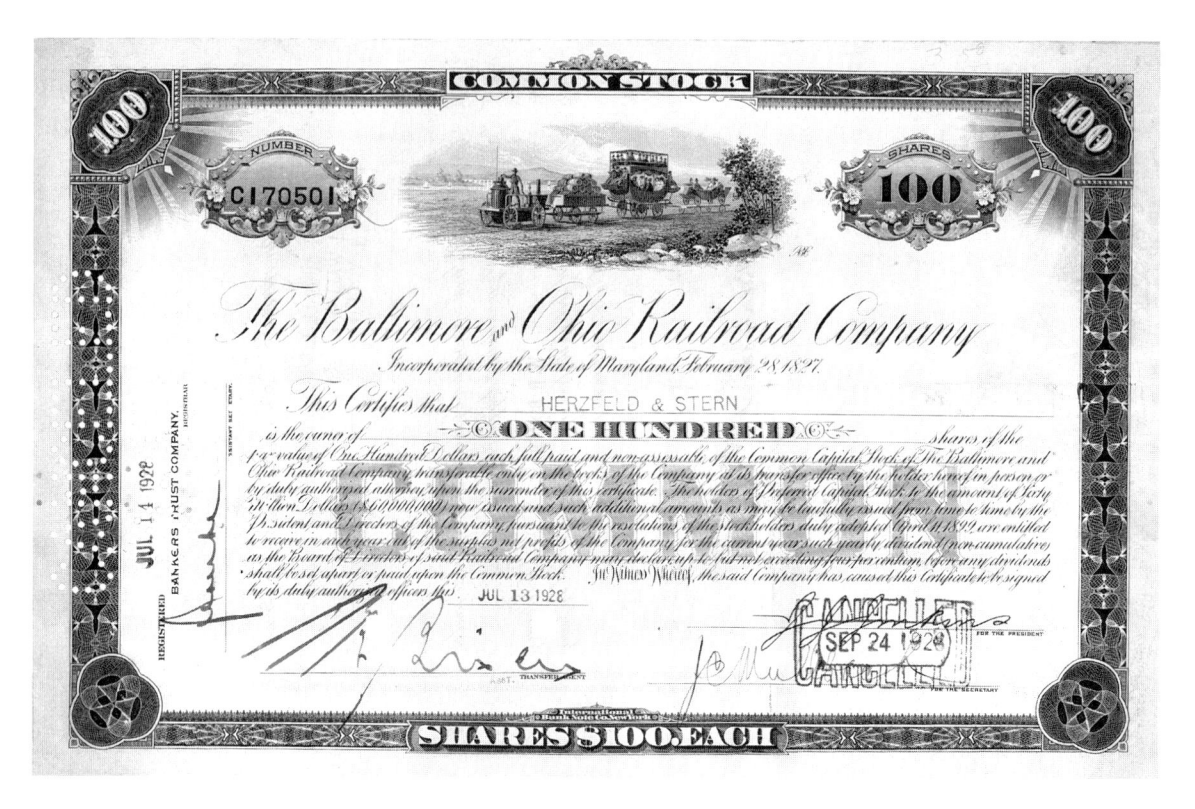

The "B&O" was America's first commercial railroad and the shares dated well after its formation portray the earliest train, the "Tom Thumb" made from scrap metal and gun barrels.

The greater number, of course, are in Europe and most of these were centred on the mining areas of those countries. At least three, however, those of France, Germany and Russia, originated as playthings of their countries' rulers.

RUSSIA

Tsar Nicholas I of Russia, impressed by a visit to Britain, granted a concession to a company to build a 24km railway from St. Petersburg to Pavlovsk via the Summer Palace. Two locomotives were ordered, a Stephenson and a Hackworth, and on arrival were promptly baptized by the Greek Orthodox Church. A somewhat bizarre beginning for what is now the largest single railway system in the world. But it is interesting to note that even this small line was profitable, generating a 4% dividend in 1839 and 7% in 1856.

The first significant line in Russia was the Warsaw-Vienna railway (Warsaw being under Russian control at that time), which was completed in 1848. After this date progress was swift and the completion of the Moscow-St. Petersburg line, later renamed the Nicolas Railway (now the October Railway), set the tone for future development. Many newly-formed railway companies were financed by foreign capital with funds coming from Britain, France, Belgium, Germany and Holland. The amount of money involved, raised through the issue of shares and bonds, was so vast that the debts soon had to be guaranteed by the State in order to reassure foreign investors, but in the end to no avail. Defaulted Russian railway bonds are of such complexity and quantity that they now offer the scripophilist a fascinating challenge.

THE UNITED STATES OF AMERICA

Seemingly quite independent of the activities in Europe, and shortly before the opening of the Liverpool and Manchester Railway, the United States entered the field.

The Baltimore and Ohio Railway Co. was incorporated in 1827. Charles Carroll, a director of the company (and at the time the sole surviving signatory of the Declaration of Independence) turned the first spade of earth in 1828. The train, named 'Tom Thumb', was designed and built from an assortment of scrap metal, using gun barrels for boiler tubes. The first stretch of the line from Baltimore to Ellicotts Mills was opened in January 1830 and in August a race was arranged between train and horse. Horse won, but only just.

From that time on, the race to open up new lines began, but it was not until the 1850s that rapid

In 1872 the organizers of the Kentucky & Great Eastern Railway ordered $2,190,000 worth of ornately engraved bonds from the American Banknote Company with the intention of building a line between the coal and iron mines of Eastern Kentucky and West Virginia. As a central vignette they chose Daniel Boone, one of the famous pioneers who helped settle Kentucky in the 1760s and 1770s. Simon Kenton, also pictured, saved Boone's life three times during an Indian attack. The line, unfortunately, was never built!

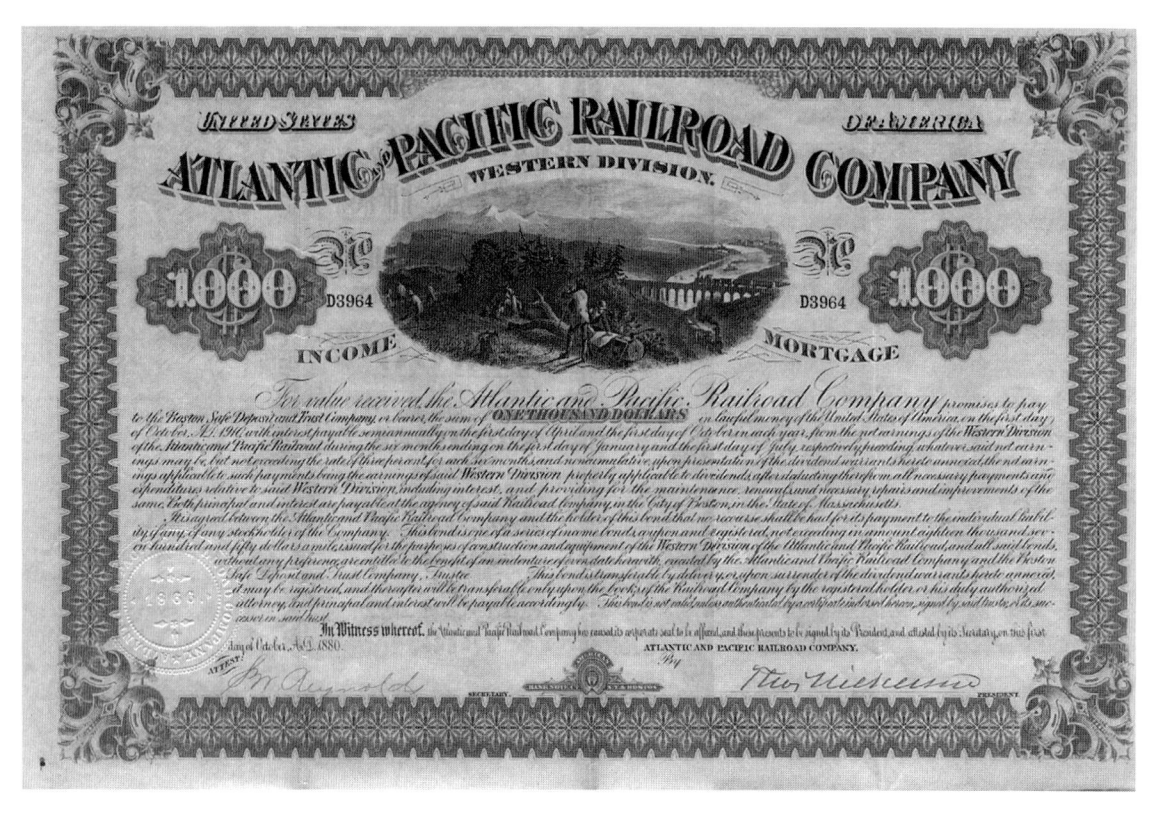

Atlantic & Pacific Railroad $1000 Income Mortgage Bond. The interest on Income Mortgage Bonds is only payable if there are net revenues after expenses. These bonds were issued to finance the construction of 575 miles of track between Albuquerque and the Colorado River.

progress was made. The difficult terrain and varied weather conditions of the USA emphasized the inadequacies and unreliability of the early steam engines. The Chicago and Rock Island RR was the first to reach the Mississippi in 1854, closely followed by the Illinois Central and the Chicago and Alton. Despite often violent objections by the rivermen, the river was finally bridged in 1856.

The Civil War of 1861 spurred Lincoln into the joining of east and west and so preventing any possible breakaway by the West Coast states. The Central Pacific RR of California was incorporated in 1861 and the following year saw the launch of the Union Pacific RR. But it was not until May 1869 that the two great lines met at Promontory, Utah — now a famous tourist attraction.

Overall there were in excess of 9,000 different railroad companies operating in the United States. Many were eventually merged into groups controlled by the railway barons such as Gould, Vanderbilt and Drew. The story of the Erie Railroad gives some idea of the excitement and financial chicanery of the period.

THE ERIE

The "New York & Erie Railroad", as it was originally known, was New York's first through line to the West. Despite an initial grant of $3 million form the State, vast amounts of additional funding was needed, much of which came from London.

Any enterprise of this size with huge profit potential inevitably attracted the schemers of the age. The "schemers" in this case were Jim Fisk, Daniel Drew and Jay Gould on one side and Cornelius Vanderbilt on the other. The ensuing battle became one of the most infamous in economic history.

The Railroad Barons

A surprisingly small number of men came to dominate the railroads. Among these, Jay Gould was one of the most celebrated learning much of his craft from Daniel Drew, an ex-cattle drover who described himself as the first great Wall Street "speckilator" and who, despite making millions in his lifetime, died a pauper. The combined resources of Jim Fisk's bravado, Drew's wiliness and Gould's skill presented the domineering Vanderbilt with one of his greatest obstacles in controlling the railways of Eastern America.

The Battle for Control

Drew began buying Erie stock in the early 1850s and soon acquired sufficient to gain a seat on the board much to the horror of his fellow directors. Three years later he was appointed Treasurer and loaned the company $3.5 million secured on unissued stock and convertible bonds. Fortune number one soon followed as he sold stock short in a rising market and then offloaded 58,000 shares causing the price to collapse 50%.

It was at this time that Commodore Vanderbilt entered the scene appreciating the importance of establishing a railroad entrance to New York City (replacing steamboats). He started by taking control of the New York & Harlem closely followed by the New York Central. As compensation for acquiring the latter he awarded himself $6 million cash as a "kind of bonus". Next target was the Erie and his agents began purchasing stock.

Jay Gould's signature on an Erie Railroad stock is most unusual and valuable as was demonstrated by the high price achieved for this item sold in a London auction in 1992 for £6500 ($10,000).

The Pine Creek Railway constituted a 75 mile line from Stokesdale Junction to Newbury, Pennsylvania. The $1000 bond pictured is signed by William K. Vanderbilt (grandson of the Commodore) and Chauncey Depew, right hand man in the Vanderbilt empire.

Panic!

Soon Drew was removed from the board and all seemed to be going to plan until Drew decided to call his loan and convert his "convertible bonds" into stock promptly dumping 100,000 new shares onto the market. The result came to be known as the "Erie Panic" causing all railroad shares to crash. Vanderbilt cried foul and arranged for the appointment of a receiver but not before Fisk, Drew and Gould raided the reserves and sailed across the Hudson to New Jersey accompanied by $6 million in "greenbacks"! The three were pursued and set up their base surrounded by thugs at "Fort Taylor", the local hotel.

After major verbal battles fought through the press and many payoffs, the "war" ended with some compensation being paid to the Commodore but control of the Erie lay firmly in the hands of Gould and Fisk. They purchased the Opera House as a new company headquarters with company funds, but somehow had themselves registered as the owners. It was promptly leased to the Erie for $75,000 per month.

The end result was the demise of a once great railroad. In 1872 Fisk was shot dead in a lover's quarrel and Gould was eventually toppled from his 'eyrie'. Their mismanagement and asset squandering left the company with $64 million of debt, a load so onerous that no dividends were paid for 69 years!

Penn Central Corporation

For some reason, the Erie never found its way into that other famous grouping of Eastern railroads, the Penn Central Corporation.

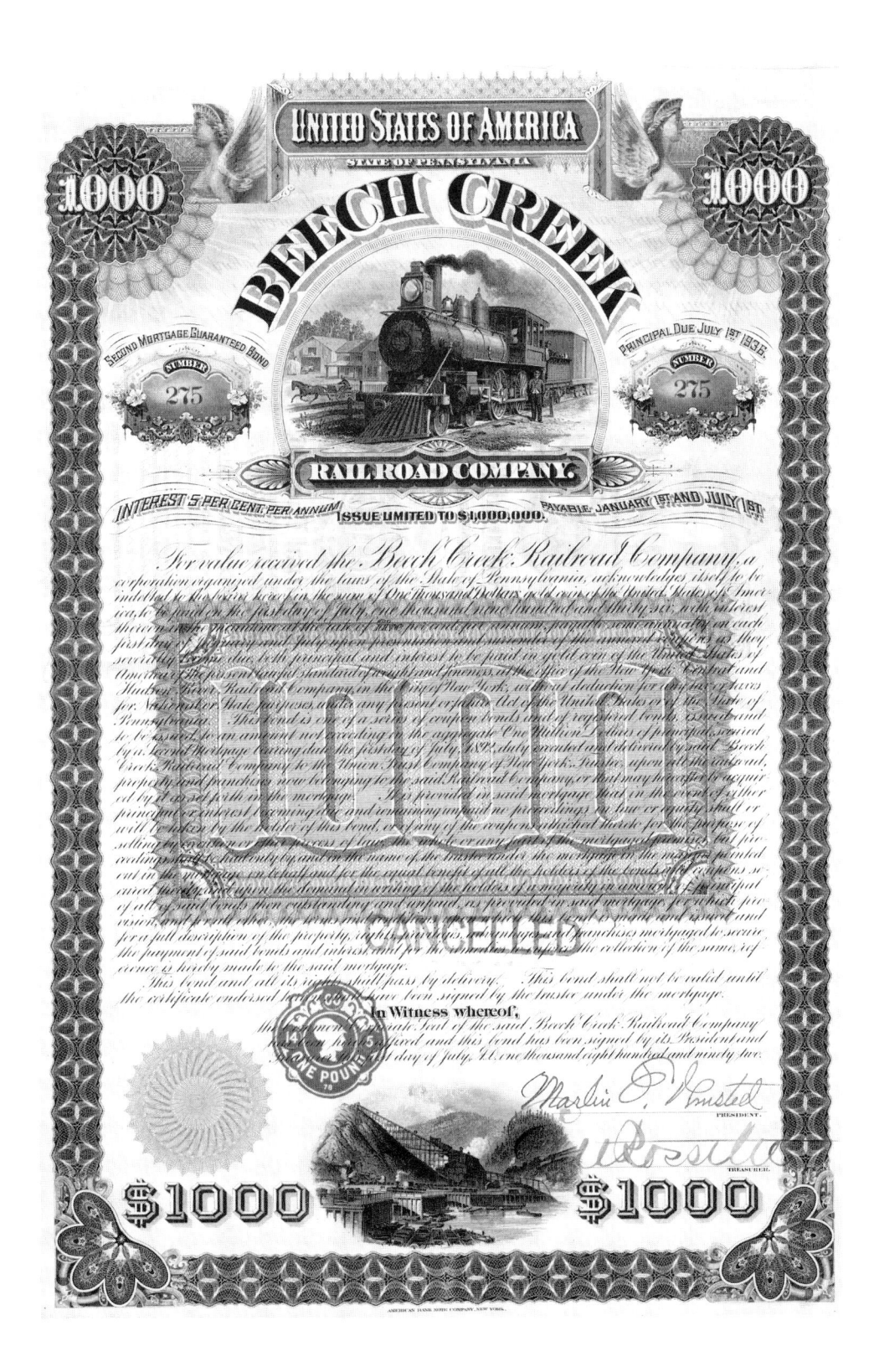

Originally incorporated in 1898, the Beech Creek Railroad was leased to the New York Central & Hudson River RR Company in 1890 for 999 years. Eventually it became part of Penn Central.

Between its incorporation in 1846 and its financial reorganisation in 1970, Penn Central became the foremost railroad operator in the Eastern United States. The original line, opened in 1850, extended 250 miles from Harrisburg to Pittsburgh. Over the ensuing years the "Pennsylvania Railroad Company" and its later partner, the "New York Central", gradually acquired by lease or purchase most of the railroad companies operating in Pennsylvania and the neighbouring States.

Amazingly, many of the stocks and bonds relating to those absorbed companies survived, having been carefully stored by the registrar. Consequently, a major group of railroads are now widely available to the collector, many bearing signatures of the early Barons including Vanderbilt, Morgan and Harriman.

CHINA

Some mention has already been made of the railway bonds of China but it may be interesting to comment on the early beginnings.

It was not until 1876 that the Chinese risked the new mode of transport and, even then, a ten-mile railway from Shanghai to Woosung, designed and built by British engineers, was viewed with constant suspicion — a suspicion finally 'confirmed' by the death of a Chinaman run down by the 'smoking dragon'. As a result, the Government took over the railway, ripped it up and dumped it somewhere in Formosa (now Taiwan).

Five years later, C. W. Kinder surreptitiously constructed a track at Kaiping to transport coal. The engine was locally made and named 'The Rocket of China'. Even that nomenclature could not save it from the government inspector, who promptly had it buried. It was later exhumed and put back into service.

Although during the latter part of the 1880s China built a few short lines, within ten years it was once again issuing concessions to foreigners. One of the most important of these was the building of the Chinese Eastern Railway by the Russians in 1897.

The railway system progressed and by about 1907 it was possible to travel from London to the Far East in a little over two weeks via the Trans-Siberian and the Chinese Eastern Railways. Agreements to build a new line often took years of negotiation. The Canton-Kowloon Railway, for example, was first proposed in 1899 as being a vital ingredient for the prosperity of Hong Kong, but it was 1907 before construction work began and 1911 before completion.

Following the 1911 revolution and the removal of the Emperor, the Chinese Government endeavoured to bring all the railways under their control. Foreign funds were still used, but the railways were constructed and managed by Chinese with the assistance of foreign technicians. From around 1925 the railways fell completely under Chinese jurisdiction, but despite this Europe continued to be the main source of finance, as evidenced by the many foreign bonds.

SOUTH AMERICA

The somewhat chaotic nature of South American railways stems from their haphazard development. Most were built relatively recently and usually financed by foreign investors. The bonds issued to finance their construction can be extremely attractive and many are finely engraved by Waterlow (Brazil Railway) or Bradbury Wilkinson (Salvador Railway).

The story of the Costa Rica Railway makes interesting reading.

The Costa Rica Railway

The man behind the project was an American, Minor Cooper Keith, whose mother was the sister of Henry Meiggs, the builder of the Callao Lima & Oraeja Railway in Peru.

The Canton-Kowloon Railway is still the main link between Hong Kong and mainland China. The bonds issued to finance its construction were issued in 1908 and remained in default for almost 50 years

Built to transport coffee in the 1880s, the Salvador Railway still flourishes. The debentures issued to finance construction carry the names of the towns through which the line runs. Engraved by banknote printers Bradbury Wilkinson.

Keith obtained a contract from the Costa Rican Government to construct a line to transport coffee from Limon on the coast to the capital, San Jose. It took three years to cover the first 70 miles through some of the most difficult terrain in the world, despite an experienced workforce which had been largely drawn from early Panama Canal excavations. Lack of funds forced Keith to travel to London to persuade the British to invest in the railway, a task made doubly difficult by Costa Rica's default on its foreign bonds. Negotiations resulted in the formation of the "Costa Rica Railway Company" in 1886 which was empowered to take over the partly finished line and to complete the project.

Two debenture issues were authorised amounting to £1.2 million, the proceeds of which were paid to Keith together with one third of the company's equity. In addition the company was granted a lease on 800,000 acres of land alongside the railway. The portrait of the President of Costa Rica, Bernardo Soto, who did much to encourage construction, appears prominently on the debentures. The line was finally opened in 1891 and runs to this day.

Minor Cooper Keith continued to build railways in Guatamala and Salvador, eventually consolidating those interests in the "International Railways of Central America", but his main claim to fame proved to be bananas! The land provided by the Costa Rican Government was used to establish banana plantations which proved so profitable that a separate company was formed (the "Tropical Trading & Transport Company"). Clashes with a rival company, the "Boston Fruit Company" resulted in a merger and the creation of the all powerful "United Fruit Company" — an organisation with such influence that it gave rise to the expression "Banana Republics"!

SOUTH AFRICA

Prior to the discovery of diamonds in 1869 and gold in 1886 there was little need for, or interest in, railways in South Africa. But with the changed economy the race to develop communications became frantic. Cecil Rhodes succeeded in extending the Cape Government Railway northward from Kimberley and in 1892 the first train reached Johannesburg. Following the Boer War and the formation of the Union in 1910 considerable efforts were made to consolidate the various lines and in 1916 the three major systems of the Central South African Railways, the Cape Government Railways, and the Natal Government Railways, merged.

President Bernardo Soto is portrayed on this impressive debenture raised to finance construction of the Costa Rica Railway. Interestingly the debenture is made out to one of the Murrieta brothers, famous financiers of many South American projects of a doubtful nature.

AUTOMOBILES

Following the successful development of steam railways, it is not surprising the next step was development of a horseless road vehicle. This time it was France, not Britain, where most early progress was made and the reason was simply a legal one. Whereas Britain imposed a 10 mph speed limit and a requirement for a red flag to be carried ahead of the vehicle, France was more liberal.

Thus, although the first petrol driven car was produced by Daimler in 1887, it was France which rapidly took the lead in building commercial quantities of vehicles. The most prominent manufacturer of the time was Panhard and Levassor, whose factory in Paris was the pride of the industry, employing 850 men by 1901. Other early French companies included such famous names as 'Mors' and 'De Dion-Bouton', while 'Minerva Motors' established its reputation in building engines and conversion kits for the bicycle.

Progress was surprisingly fast in the first few years and this was greatly encouraged by the establishment of 'races'. The first of these in 1894 was sponsored by the French newspaper Le Petit Journal, which announced 'a competition for carriages to be propelled without horses'. The course

Direct Drive Motor Company. Organized in Philadelphia and active between 1919-1924, the company built automobiles in Pottsdown, Pennsylvania, and sold them under the name "Champion". The name Direct-Drive derived from the drive system which consisted of groove rings on the rear wheels meshed with grooved pulleys on each end of a jackshaft.

Mestre & Blatge. Fine looking French automobile share of the 1920s.

was from Paris to Rouen and entry required an ability to achieve 7¾ miles per hour. Only three contestants lasted the course, averaging 12 mph. But it was the following year which really set the standards with the inauguration of the Paris-Bordeaux-Paris race, a distance of 732 miles. Twenty-two cars took part and nine finished — a significant improvement over the previous year.

In Britain, meanwhile, attitudes were mellowing and not only was the red flag abolished but the speed limit was raised to 14 miles per hour! To celebrate, supporters organized a procession of cars travelling from London to Brighton in 1896, and so began the famous annual event. By 1913 nearly 200 British companies were producing cars but most failed. Much of the interest in early automotive transport, not surprisingly perhaps, came from the wealthy. Such worthies as W. K. Vanderbilt, Baron Henri de Rothschild and the Hon. C. S. Rolls were active participants in races of the time. One such event, first organized in 1900, was the Gordon-Bennet Cup, named after the wealthy newspaper proprietor. This race attracted enormous publicity and greatly encouraged competition at both the national and corporate level. A rule of entry insisted on manufacture being one hundred per cent of the country whose flag was represented.

The concentration of early development in France resulted in the adoption of several French words into the automobile vocabulary. 'Automobile' itself is an obvious one and others include 'garage', 'chauffeur' and 'mechanic'. Manufacturing was not limited to Europe, during the first four months of

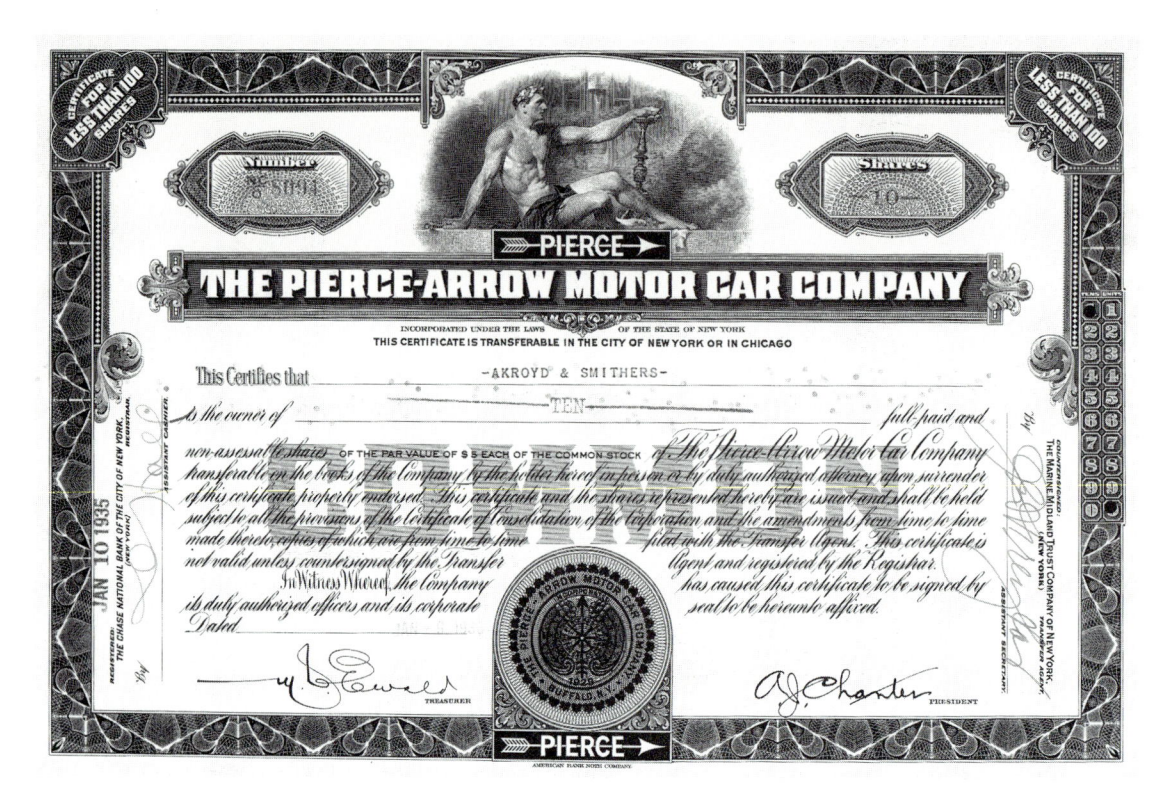

Pierce-Arrow was one of the American auto pioneers. This share certificate dates from 1938.

1899, 80 companies were formed in the United States with a total share capital of $338 million and by 1903 there were reputed to be 300 factories building mechanically driven road vehicles. But it was the appearance of Henry Ford on the scene which not only established American dominance of the industry but also made the car available to all, and not just the privileged.

Ford

Henry Ford began his company in partnership with 12 others in 1903 with a capital of $28,000. Buick, Pierce-Arrow, Cadillac and Packard all began around the same time and so joined the older companies, Oldsmobile, Studebaker, Haynes and Locomobile. Apart from these well known names, there were about 500 other companies formed to make cars in the United States at that time, most of which failed. In 1909 the "Model T" was born, a vehicle which dominated the market for almost 20 years. By 1914 250,000 Model Ts a year were being sold representing 45% of the US market. Ford's River Rouge plant employed 100,000 workers and stretched over 1,100 acres. But success inevitably brought competition, one of the most significant being William Durant who in 1909 started to pull together a vast combine along the lines of Standard Oil and US Steel; the result was "General Motors". Buick, Cadillac and Oldsmobile were soon absorbed and Dodge followed shortly after. Despite increasingly strong competition, the Ford Motor Company made profits of over $1 billion in its first 25 years.

Other Vehicles

Production was not limited to the private passenger vehicle, for it was seen at an early date that in order to gain widespread popularity the general public must be involved and given the opportunity to benefit from developments. An extract from an article which appeared in the London Daily Mail of 30 November 1897 indicates the thinking of the time: 'We hardly turn round now to look at the motor cab. This has been found perfectly practicable, perfectly comfortable, perfectly safe. It is now the turn of the motor omnibus, and from one quarter or another it is certain to arise before long. After that we pine for the motor dray. Meanwhile, it is not a bad year's record that half London has already left off laughing at a carriage without a horse; the other half will soon get tired of laughing when only one man in two sees the joke.' Most of the early omnibuses were manufactured by De Dion-Bouton et Cie and exported worldwide. Ready markets included Bolivia, USA, Italy, Austria and Spain. Several companies were established in Spain to run the vehicles, one of the most significant being the 'Sociedad Espanola de Automoviles Segovie a la Granja', which made a point of allocating one of its vehicles for the sole use of the Royal Family. Many of the old omnibus company share certificates exist today and make fascinating collecting material.

Daimler-Benz, one of the most famous names in the automobile world, was formed in 1925 as a result of a merger between Benz Rheinische Automobile-und Mortoren-fabrik of Mannheim and Daimler Motoren-Gesellschaft of Stuttgart. Modern shares of Daimler-Benz picture the two founders, Gottlieb Daimler and Carl Benz, who despite working within two hours of each other, never met.

All new technology has military uses and as early as 1902 prototype armed tanks were being prepared. First attempts were little more than 'cars' surrounded by steel sheeting with guns on top. The earliest such vehicle was designed by Fred R. Simms and built by Vickers, Son & Maxim Ltd., but its first trial was not attended by the army, as The Autocar magazine of 1902 somewhat cynically put it: 'Doubtless they (the War Office) were most intensely employed in the design of some fresh form of dustman's cap, wherewith to further disfigure the Guards and alienate the nursemaid's heart. Such important matters must not be put aside for the consideration of such an airy and insignificant trifle as "Simm's motor war car".' Bureaucracy, it appears, is nothing new.

It may come as a surprise to discover Charlie Chaplin in a book on scripophily, but his film success resulted in the formation of several business ventures, this one with his brother Sydney, to whom the share illustrated is made out. Signed by Charlie Chaplin as President.

SIGNATURES

Famous signatures not only enhance a certificate from an historical point of view, but can also appreciably affect its value as discussed later. Recognizing a signature is not always easy and a well informed collector can often pick up a bargain at a dealer's expense. In order to give a feel for the theme, several of the better-known signatories are dealt with in some depth in the pages which follow, while others are listed on page 114.

Most shares certificates of the early American Express Company were signed by Henry Wells and William Fargo, two of the company's founders. This one is dated 1859 ("Type II"). Certificates issued in the 1860s have the "Dog" logo rather than a train.

WELLS AND FARGO

Perhaps of all the internationally well known signatories to be found on early share certificates, those of Henry Wells and William Fargo are the most coveted. To many they are synonymous with the opening up of the American West.

Henry Wells, an ex-schoolteacher and son of a pastor, learnt the express business under William F. Harnden ('the father of express') and in 1841 formed Pomeroy & Co., which not only carried valuables and currency but, for a while, even oysters (at $3 per 100) and mail, much to the government's dismay. The business was centred on Buffalo.

In 1843 Wells met and hired W. G. Fargo as a messenger and shortly afterwards formed a partnership, running an express line from Buffalo to Detroit. Eventually many of the competing companies joined forces and in March 1850 the American Express Company was formed with a capital of $150,000. It was an unincorporated association with a limited life of only ten years. Shares were first offered to the public in 1853 but a special provision prevented anyone from buying shares in the company without the board's consent, and shares could not be sold to "married women, infants or irresponsible persons". Shares from 1853 are extremely rare.

Many agreements were established with the railroad and packet boat companies. Wells was appointed President at an annual salary of $1,250, and in its first four months the Company earned enough to pay a 10% dividend on capital. In 1852 Wells and Fargo wanted to expand operations to California and cash in on the gold rush, but other directors opposed the idea. As a result a new offshoot was created — "The Wells Fargo Company", which became the leading express company in the West. Another equally famous offshoot, "The Overland Mail", was set up by fellow director John Butterfield, running stage coaches from St. Louis to San Francisco.

By 1854 the Company had increased its capital to $750,000. Business developed fast and their messengers covered 15,000 miles a day. Headquarters were established in New York and a spur track from the Hudson River Railroad Co. ran right into the ground floor permitting direct loading and unloading.

After its first ten years, and in accordance with the original terms, the Company was dissolved and the assets auctioned off. Existing shareholders successfully bid for them at a cost of $600,000.

In 1867 a major competitor was formed by a group of wealthy businessmen known as the 'Merchants Union Express Co.' The resulting price war led to both companies making substantial losses and they finally agreed to merge, forming the 'American Merchants Union Express Co.' Wells resigned as President and was succeeded by Fargo, although his younger brother, J. C. Fargo, handled most of the detail. The name was changed back to the American Express Co. in 1873 and J. C. Fargo became President in 1881.

The development of the company with its gradually increasing capitalization is clearly depicted by the share certificates and at least ten different designs have been identified. Both Wells and Fargo signatures appear on the certificates, but only that of Fargo on the American Merchants Union Express Co., Wells having by then retired.

JOHN D. ROCKEFELLER

Born in 1839, the son of a patent medicine salesman, John D. Rockefeller built up one of the largest personal fortunes in history.

Like all great entrepreneurs, his success arose from a modest outlay on a new product — that product just happened to be oil. An initial $4,000 investment in a refinery in 1862 was the start of the Standard Oil Company of Ohio. In 1868, Henry Flagler joined Rockefeller and by 1870 the Company was incorporated with a share capital of $1 million. All 10,000 shares were owned by Rockefeller, Andrews, Flagler and Harkness.

Refining 1,500 barrels a day, the Company became the world's largest oil producer. It rapidly acquired most of the country's refineries by fair means or foul and by 1880 controlled 90% of the US oil business. In 1882 the group was consolidated under the title "Standard Oil Trust". The powers derived from its domination of the business eventually led, through a series of anti-trust cases, to its forced break-up in 1911.

Between 1875 and 1882, when the Company increased its capital from $1 million to $3.5 million, the share certificates of the "Standard Oil Company" bear the signatures of Rockefeller and Flagler. As the number of shareholders was tightly controlled (only five in 1870 and forty-one in 1880) very few such certificates are believed to exist (estimate, around 350-400) and as a consequence tend to fetch consistently high prices at auction, usually around $10,000.

The later certificates of the "Standard Oil Trust" mostly carry Rockefellers signature but more of this type are known and prices are more modest.

Undoubtedly the most celebrated oil company, Standard Oil was the vehicle used by Rockefeller to create the world's largest monopoly. The shares are signed by Rockefeller and Flagler.

GREGOR MACGREGOR, CAZIQUE OF POYAIS

Appealing signatures do not always have to be those of upright men or women. The infamous can be as attractive as the famous; such is that of Gregor MacGregor.

A Scottish mercenary of the early nineteenth century, MacGregor rose to the rank of General in the Venezuelan army under Simon Bolivar. He was instrumental in the expulsion of the Spanish and together with a small force landed in a swampy mosquito-infested area of Nicaragua. There he 'negotiated' land rights with the primitive inhabitants (the "Mosquito Indians") and in 1821 sailed for England where he was able to transfix his audiences with fabulous tales of the wonderful, albeit non existent, "Kingdom of Poyais".

The discontented populace of the time were enthused by his tales of fertile soil, mineral wealth and even an opera house(!) and were soon pressing to emigrate. MacGregor, self-styled "Cazique of Poyais", began selling land grants and local currency notes, raising £200,000 in 1822 with the aid of respected London bankers Perring & Co. This was followed by a further issue of £300,000 in Paris in 1825.

Many sailed to find their Utopia well endowed with tropical heat, disease and hurricanes but little else. Despite brave attempts by the Governor of British Honduras to rescue the duped settlers, over 200 died.

In 1827 MacGregor was imprisoned in England but soon released, implying involvement of more well known establishment figures. A similar spell in a French prison was followed by his retirement to Venezuela, where he was reinstated to his former army rank and, on death, granted full military honours.

The bonds and land grants often bear the signature of Gregor MacGregor, which greatly adds to their glamour. But, signatures aside, the documents make fascinating and amusing reading and demonstrate the ease of perpetrating a fraud in a world only just entering the era of fast communications.

THE COMMODORE — CORNELIUS VANDERBILT

It would be remiss in a section devoted to famous signatures to omit reference to at least one of the great "Railway Barons".

Starting with $100 borrowed from his mother, Cornelius Vanderbilt began his career in shipping, thus adopting the title "Commodore". While in his twenties he bought his first steamship and eventually controlled a sizeable fleet ferrying people and goods around New York Harbour. Seeing the beginnings and advantages of railroads, he purchased the Harlem Railroad and extended it to Manhattan. After this came the Hudson River RR Co. and, eventually, the New York Central. His business deals bore the true marks of an entrepreneur of the time — deviousness and unscrupulousness. At his death he was the richest man in America.

His son, William Henry, and grandsons Cornelius and William Kissam, all followed the Commodore into the railroad empire. Their signatures appear on many certificates, including the New York and Harlem, the Canada Southern and the New York Central.

Space does not permit full credit to all the famous original and facsimile signatures gracing bonds and shares. Many of these are therefore only listed, but even this does not purport to be comprehensive and is only indicative of the scope of this most fascinating collecting theme.

SIGNATURE	CERTIFICATE
Henry Wells & William Fargo	American Express Co. (1852-70)
John D. Rockefeller	Standard Oil Co. (1870s)
J. Paul Getty (facsimile)	Mission Development Co (1950s)
Bernie Cornfield (facsimile)	I.O.S. (1960s)
Gregor MacGregor	Poyais (c.1820-30)
Commodore Cornelius Vanderbilt	New York & Harlem RR
Robert Morris	North American Land Co. (c.1795)
Whittaker Wright (facsimile)	London & Globe Co.
Stephen Austin	Texian Loan, 1836
Thomas A Edison	Edison Portland Cement Co. (c.1899)
Abe Bailey	Du Preez Gold Mining
Johann Strauss	Der Komische Oper
George Pullman	Pullman's Palace Car Co. (c.1869)
William Bingham	Philadelphia & Lancaster Turnpike
Thomas J Watson (Mr IBM)	Irving Trust Co. (1931)
Charlie Chaplin	Chaplin Studios Inc. (c.1918)
Nathan Rothschild	1822 Russian State Loan
Samuel F. B. Morse	New Orleans & Ohio Telegraph

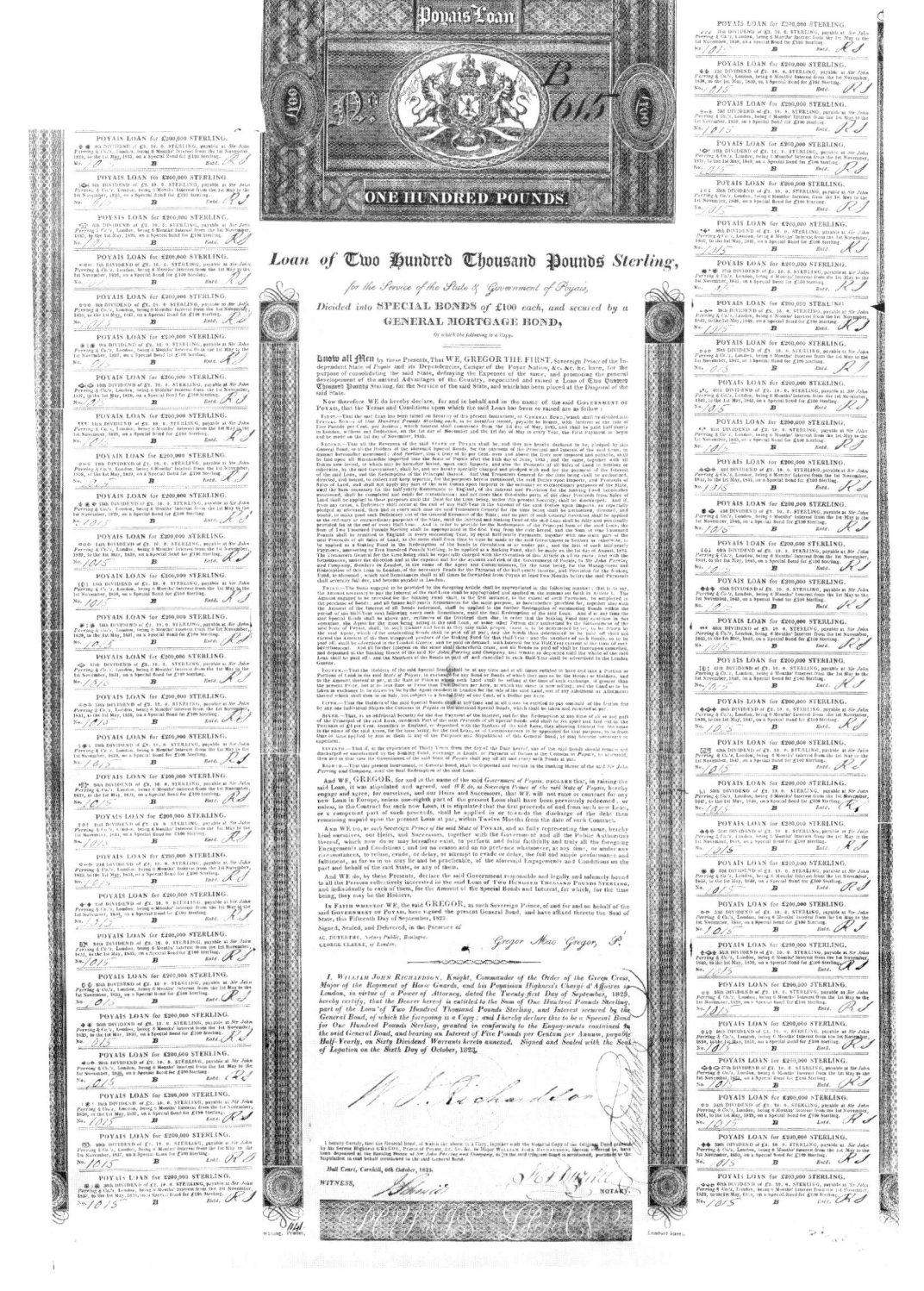

If fraud is the objective, the paperwork must look good as evidenced by this £100 bond in Gregor MacGregor's Poyais dated 1823! Note the opening words: "We, Gregor the First, sovereign prince of the independent State of Poyais." There's no point in being shy either!

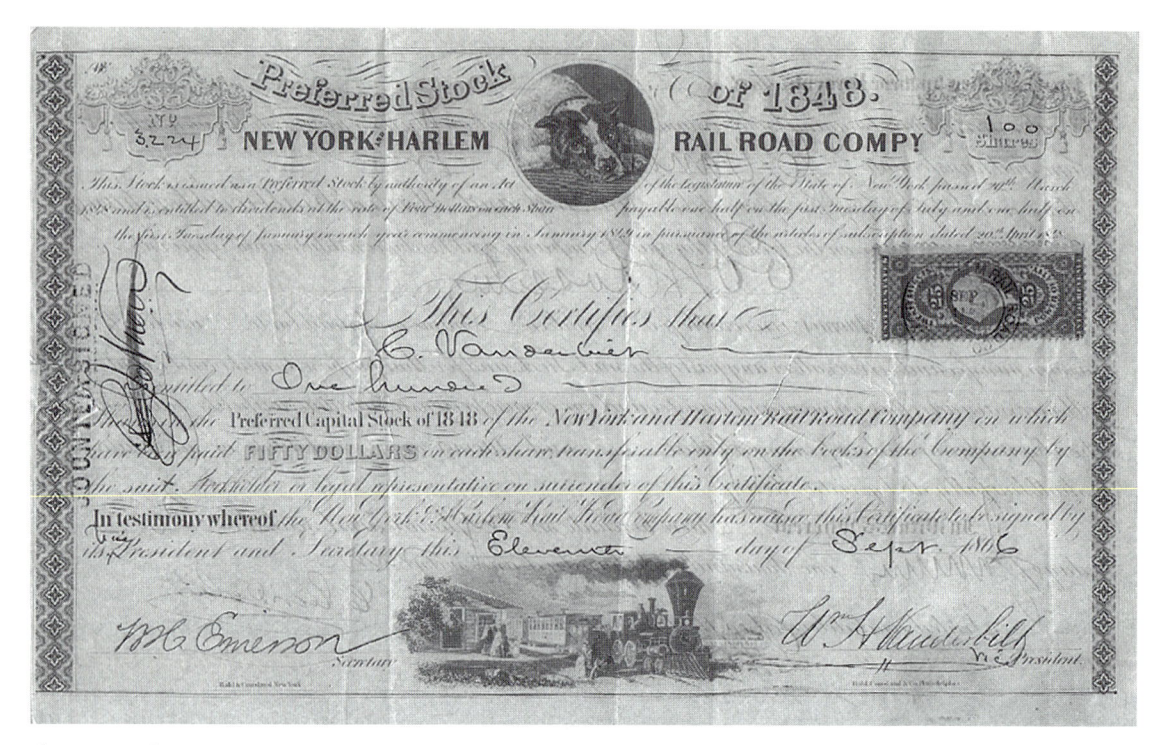

The New York & Harlem was Vanderbilt's first railroad and became the focus of many of his financial activities. This certificate is particularly interesting being made out to the "Commodore" and signed by his son, William H. Vanderbilt, as Vice President. Despite being considered inept by his father, William went on to double the family fortune.

MINING

Second only to railways in terms of volume and variety of material, mining offers the collector a vast area from which may be selected specific themes such as gold or silver or simply geographical locations.

GOLD

Throughout the centuries gold has always held a unique fascination. It has been the most sought after element, at times involving thousands of hopeful prospectors. Inevitably this constant searching resulted in the formation of many companies and the subsequent issue of a large variety of related share certificates. Although the mining of gold goes back many centuries, the issue of share certificates does not, and for that reason concentration is on the period from the mid-nineteenth century, when gold was first discovered and mined on a significant commercial scale.

The great 'Gold Rush' began in 1848 in California. Gold was discovered by James W. Marshall close by his partner's ranch at Sutters Fort. At the time, San Francisco boasted a population of 800 and it was only one year after the state of California had been transferred to America from Mexico.

News of the discovery spread fast and prospectors travelled from across the world to try their hand — they became known as the 'forty-niners' and swelled the population of California from 26,000 to 115,000 within a year. Difficulties of travel and doubts over successful discoveries on arrival led to the grouping together of the prospectors, often under the umbrella of a company. For this reason many of the companies of the period formed to mine gold in California were in fact registered elsewhere. Examples are the Ave Maria Gold Quartz Mine and the Anglo-Californian Gold Mining Co., both registered in London.

Advantages of forming a company were not only limited to a sharing of risks and rewards, but it also gave the opportunity for overseas investors, to participate at a distance.

The frantic scramble for gold in the 1850s inevitably led to social problems, many of which were racially based — a feature common to most of the major gold mining areas. However, apart from these unfortunate aspects, a great many positive features developed, one being much improved mining techniques. Although not a mining company, the share certificate of the Tuolomne County Water Co. (1854) beautifully portrays the alluvial process.

One of the early gold miners was Edward Hargraves from England, although originally from Australia. He recalled mountains of a similar shape to those being mined in California from his Australian childhood and so set off to seek them out. He discovered gold in New South Wales, Australia, in 1851. The development process was much the same as California, with frantic searching and large influxes of foreigners, but many of the techniques learnt in the United States were successfully adopted in Australia. Typical companies of the time were the British Australia Gold Mining Co. (1851) and the Lake Bathurst Australasian Gold Mining Co.

Incorporated shortly after the end of the Civil War, the President of the Selma Marion & Memphis Railroad was Nathan Bedford Forrest, famous Confederate cavalry general and first head of the Ku Klux Klan. The bond is signed by Forrest, whose autograph is comparatively rare.

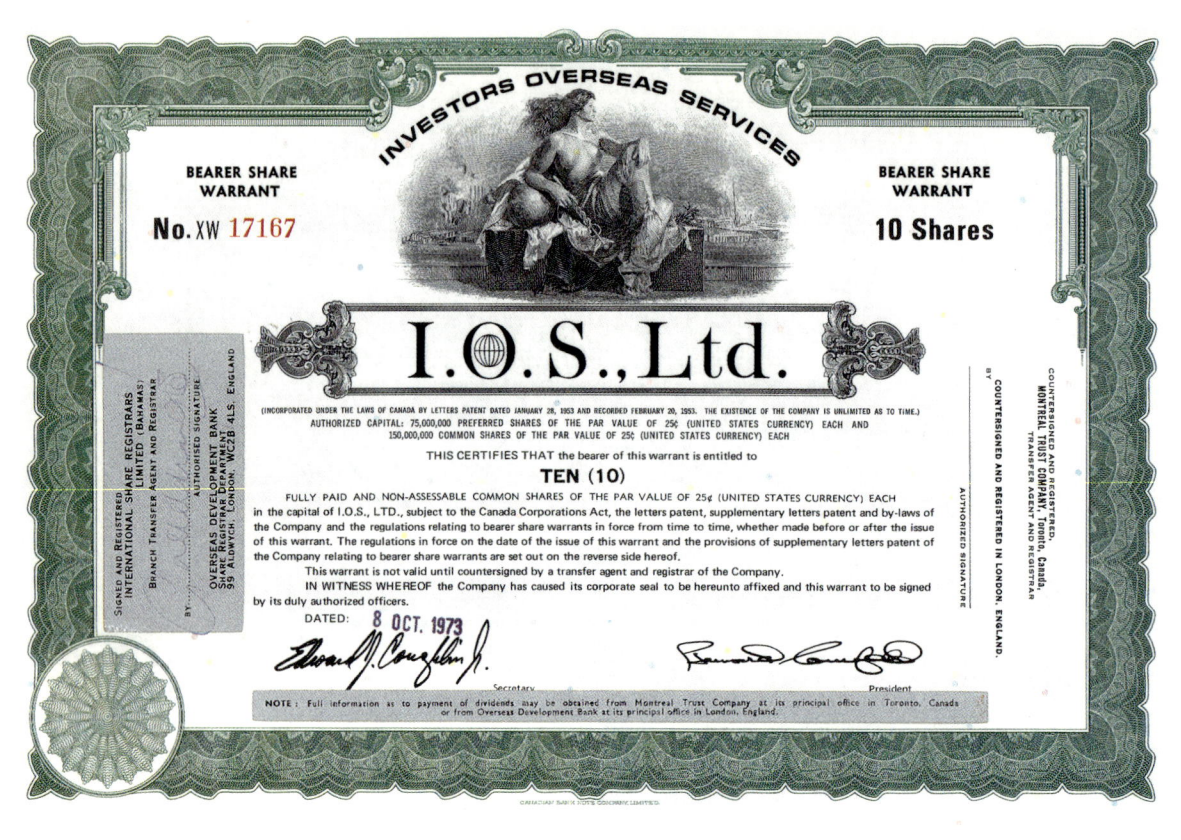

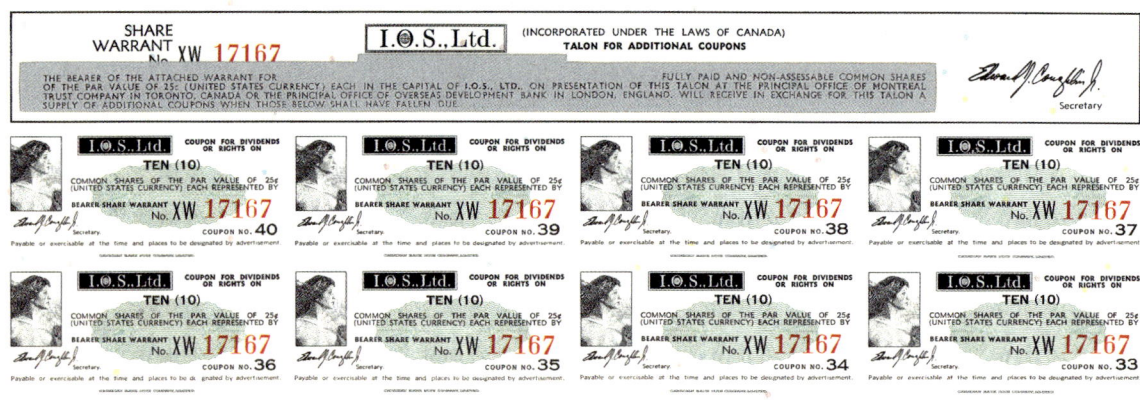

"Do You Sincerely Want to be Rich?" Original investors in IOS certainly did but unfortunately reaped little reward when the company folded. Facsimile signatures of two of the culprits Bernie Cornfield and Ed Coughlin.

The Mary Murphy Gold Mining Company. Incorporated in Colorado and dated 1909.

The third major area of discovery was South Africa. Gold was discovered at Witwatersrand, in the Transvaal, in 1886, but unlike California and Australia it was difficult and costly to mine, thus necessitating the establishment of a more organized commercial approach at an early stage. Many companies were formed and several of these have been referred to in the chapter on South Africa. The companies were mostly registered in London or on the gold fields themselves at the local stock exchanges of Kimberley and Barberton.

Gold discoveries were not limited to the three areas briefly described here and the scripophilist who chooses this theme will find fascinating material from Mexico to the Far East.

DIAMONDS

South Africa dominates diamond mining. There are relatively few certificates from other countries concerned with this theme although an interesting exception is the Societé Minière Intercoloniale of the Central African Republic. Remember those diamonds reputed to have been 'given' to a French President by Emperor Bokassa? Well, that's where they came from.

Crown United Gold Mining Company. Unusual vignette of clasped hands in mining company located in Western Australia.

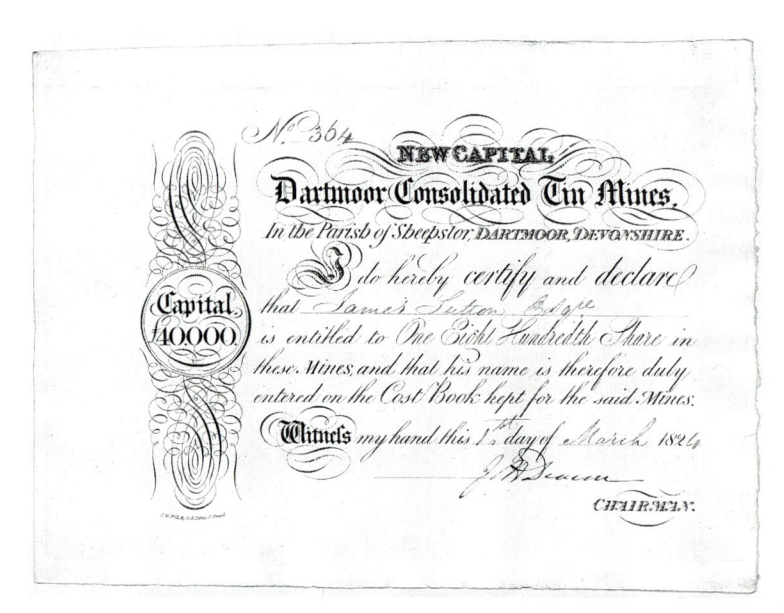

One of Cornwall's early tin mining companies dating from 1818. This share was issued in 1824.

COPPER

Copper deposits were far more common than gold or diamonds and the choice of certificates is consequently much more varied. The largest producing region in Europe in the latter part of the nineteenth century was Devon and Cornwall in Great Britain. The Devon Great Consols Mine produced over £3 million worth of ore between 1844 and 1864. Copper was also actively mined in South Africa, Australia, the United States and Scandinavia.

TIN

Without doubt the centre of tin mining in the early 1800s was Cornwall. Presence of the deposits led to the region becoming a major area of industrialization and the workings resulted in the development of much advanced equipment. One of the most significant such offshoot was steam traction and it was the son of the manager of the Dolcoath Mine, Richard Trevithick, who built the first steam locomotive.

Other tin mining areas included Nigeria, the Far East and Australia.

OTHER MINERALS

Whether your interests are with lead, silver or coal, there is no doubt that there is adequate interesting material on which to develop a collection. Mining often formed the nucleus of social and economic progress in a community and for this reason it is a particularly interesting field in which to specialize. The material is often attractive and was usually held by relatively small groups of people, thus limiting the quantities issued of individual types.

The mining company shares illustrated here will give some idea of the scope available.

BANKING

If you are one of those trusting individuals who implicitly believe in the infallibility and exclusivity of banks you may think that there will be little material for the collector. One statistic might alter that view; since 1700 over 3,120 banks have been registered in the United Kingdom alone. Most, of course, crashed, amalgamated or disappeared, but nevertheless all would have raised capital through the issue of share certificates, debentures or other financial instruments. With the addition of other countries, particularly the United States, France, Germany, Russia and South Africa, the total number of banks facing the potential collector may well exceed 2-3,000.

A couple of country backgrounds may help illustrate the field.

The Russian Colliery Company was incorporated in England like many industrial enterprises which operated in Russia.

The Ruhr was not Germany's only coal mining area, as demonstrated by this founders' share in the Schader Coal Mining Company, dated 1860. These mines were located in Saxony, near Zwickau, and were operational until the 1960s.

RUSSIA

A great many banks operated in Russia prior to the Revolution. The two most well known were the Peasants Land Bank and the Land Bank of the Nobility. Each was concerned with the problems of transferring land from nobility to serfs, although from different sides of the fence, and both were major issuers of bonds subsequently defaulted in 1917. As may be considered appropriate, the Nobility's default exceeded the Peasants' by a ratio of about 9:1, and together they accounted for nearly £100 million of Russia's total 1917 default.

One particularly interesting story concerns the 5 trading banks which controlled Russian grain finance. The story highlights the close relationship of scripophily and history — in this case, history of political intrigue.

During the latter days of World War I, considerable concern was being expressed by Britain that the Russian war effort against Germany was in danger of collapse as the Revolution began to take hold. British officers were sent to Russia with three objectives: one — to keep allied armaments out of German hands; two — to ensure continued supplies of funds to the one remaining loyal fighting unit — the Cossacks; and three — to do everything possible to ensure continuing close commercial ties with Russia after the war.

The British envoy presented with this task was General Poole who conceived a plan to take over the Russian economy through the purchase of five banks: the Russian Bank for Foreign Trade, the

Germany's first National bank, the Reichsbank, was founded in 1871 and as with many central banks was initially funded by private capital. This share is dated 1925 and shows the original headquarters which were destroyed during the Second World War. During the 1960s all private shares were bought in and the bank exists today under its present title, the Deutsche Bundesbank, one of the foremost central banks in the world.

International Bank, the Commercial and Industrial Bank, the Volga-Kana Bank, and the Bank of Siberia.

The takeover plan was approved by the British Government and funds were approved, but implementation was upset by Bolshevik suspicions, the Germans trying to do the same thing, and the tendency for large sums of money to 'go missing'. At the end of the day majority shareholdings were achieved in two of the target banks and a deposit of £300,000 paid on the Siberian Bank with an agreement to pick up the balance after the war. The overall objective was to control the Russian grain trade and thus the economy.

The Revolution put a stop to these intrigues and the banks' assets were confiscated by the State. The tale does not end there, however, for the owner of the Bank of Siberia turned up in London after the war and demanded the agreed balance of £3 million for his shares. The Treasury paid up!

UNITED STATES

The first bank to be incorporated was the "Bank of North America" (see page 82) in 1781. It proved

Three shares in the Bank of Siberia, once keenly sought after by the British Government in 1917. The bank was active in the grain trade and its shares depict the peoples of Siberia.

to be particularly hardy and continued under various charters until well into the nineteenth century. The first attempt at a central bank was Alexander Hamilton's "Bank of the United States" which was incorporated in 1791 under a 20 year charter (it was quite usual for early US companies to be chartered for limited periods of 10 or 20 years at the outset). The Bank was under the control of the Treasury despite its minority shareholding of 20%. Operations were clearly successful judging by its results; the shares yielded an 8% return and at the end of its life original shareholders were returned 150% of their capital. But early banks were generally regarded with suspicion and no attempt was made to renew the charter after its expiry in 1811 and it was another 5 years before the next central bank was formed.

A large number of state banks sprang up in the early part of the nineteenth century and by 1815 as

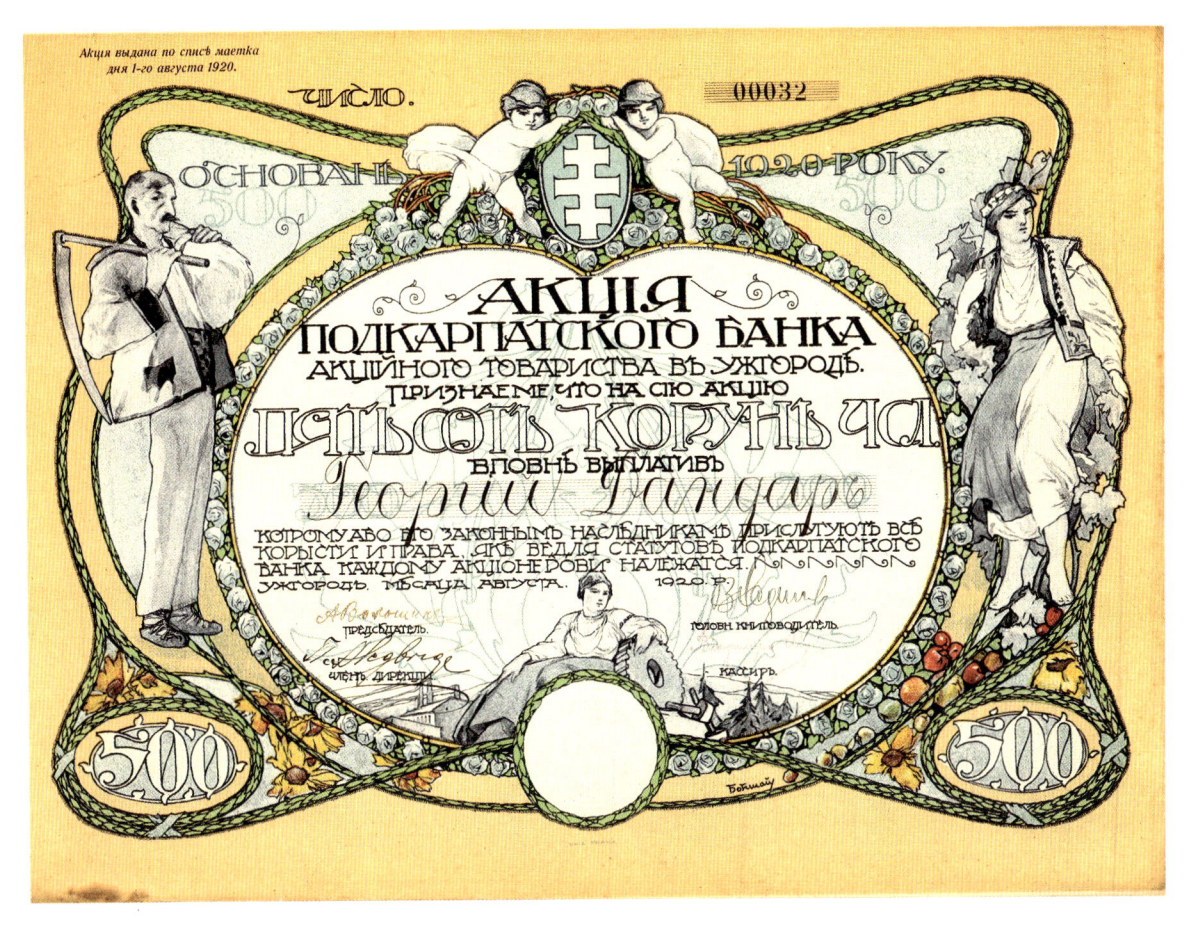

Located at Uszgerod in the Carpathian mountains, Carpathian Bank shares demonstrate how contemporary artistic styles can reach the most unusual places. Although now in Ukraine the area frequently crossed frontiers being close to the Czechoslovakian border.

many as 208 were in operation.

At a later date the effect of restrictive US banking laws which prohibited cross-state banking resulted in the formation of a large number of local institutions. Poor communications compounded this number and the result was the establishment of many small (one branch) community banks, or "savings and loans", hundreds of which still exist today often owned and run by a local family.

The collector is thus presented with a wide choice. Names such as the Bank of Charleston, the Barnstable Bank or the Morris Canal and Banking Co. are just three of many. Like all American material, the certificates are attractively printed and often carry the signatures of famous financiers.

J. P. Morgan

No section on American banking would be complete without reference to John Pierpont Morgan. Coming from a wealthy family J P Morgan began his banking career with his father's firm George Peabody & Co (later to become J S Morgan & Co and eventually, Morgan, Grenfell & Co). In 1861 he set up his own bank "J P Morgan & Co" and worked closely with Anthony Drexel. Both men became deeply involved in the railroads with Morgan able to use his British connections to sell stock outside of the United States, thus protecting the local share price. Such operations brought him close to Vanderbilt and ultimately a seat on the board of the New York Central.

J. P. Morgan signed a few certificates and this one only on the back as Trustee. The New Jersey Junction Railroad was incorporated in 1886 and provided facilities and connections for traffic interchange between several railway systems terminating at Jersey City, Hoboken and Weehawken.

Morgan reorganised numerous railroad companies and in 1895, at the request of the US Government arranged a $65 million loan which effectively stemmed a financial panic — it also netted him and his associates a tidy $16 million! His involvement with Thomas Edison resulted in the formation of General Electric and his interest in the steel industry resulted in the creation of the giant US Steel Corporation. With equity stakes in nearly all the major banking houses, Morgan became a dominant financial figure and his bank, now named Morgan Guaranty, a household name. He died in 1913 one of the wealthiest men in America.

Unlike fellow railroad barons, Morgan appears to have signed surprisingly few stocks and bonds. Because of this, prices can be high.

OTHER COUNTRIES

"Banks" is a great theme for the collector to really get to grips with. Apart from the countries mentioned here, material is available from across the world and particularly interesting items from Central Europe, South America, North Africa and the Middle East can add much to a collection.

Banco Espanol del Rio de la Plata. Impressive South American bank share depicting arms of Spain and Argentina.

Designed not to be easily mislaid, shares of the Banque de Cochinchine are stunning items.

Incorporated in 1868, the Detroit & Cleveland operated passenger and freight liners in the Great Lakes.

SHIPPING

Perhaps the oldest form of transport, shipping offers the collector a superb variety of material from across the world. Like railways, shipping companies proved to be prolific users of capital, particularly with the arrival of steam which is where our theme begins.

THE BIRTH OF STEAM

Although early experiments were carried out in France at the end of the seventeenth century, it was in Britain, or, to be more exact, Scotland, where the most significant developments took place. In 1787 W. Miller published a thesis on alternatives to wind and although his initial solution was paddle wheels driven by manpower, his associate, James Taylor, developed the idea and substituted a steam engine. The first successful test took place in 1788 on Dalswinton Loch, Scotland, where a speed of 5 mph was achieved.

In the United States, Robert Fulton, having witnessed the Scottish experiments, built the Clermont, a successful steamer which regularly plied the Hudson River between Albany and New York, a distance of 142 miles, in 32 hours. Henry Bell built a similar ship in 1812, the Comet, which sailed the Clyde from Glasgow. After this date, many ships were built on the Clyde and cross-channel services to Ireland began in 1816. A major improvement was the substitution of a screw propeller for the paddle wheel and this development was crucial in persuading the Admiralty to adopt steam driven ships for the British Royal Navy.

The close relationship between ship builders and shipping line managers stemmed from those early days in Scotland and the stories of both Cunard and the Elder Dempster Company are perfect examples of pioneering development. The tales are made more interesting for the scripophilist by the availability of share certificates in the companies and their associates.

CUNARD

Coming from a once wealthy Philadelphia family which was banished to Nova Scotia for supporting the British, Samuel Cunard created a shipping line in a manner which rivals many of the railroad barons. Setting up their new home in Halifax, the young Samuel determined to make his living from the sea and by 1812 he and his father had acquired their first schooner. Their shipping business did well as a "neutral" carrier during the wars with France, but after 1815, Halifax was no longer a garrison town and new business was needed. Cunard sought and obtained contracts from the British Post Office to carry mail to and from Bermuda and more significantly won a contract from the East India Company to receive and tranship tea from China.

Investments in a whaling fleet, the "Halifax Banking Company", local canals and the "Annapolis Mining Company" all contributed to the creation of a diverse and sizeable business empire. But it was the prospect of steam ships which really fired the imagination of Cunard, particularly the possibilities of Atlantic crossings. Such ideas were encouraged by a ride on the Liverpool & Manchester Railway and news of the first Atlantic steam crossing by a Dutch ship, the Curacao. Later crossings by the better known Great Western and the Sirius in 1838 led directly to Cunard's determination to win the Post Office contract to carry trans-Atlantic mail. Once won, he then ordered the ships, and only then set about raising the money. His "British & North American Royal Mail Steam Packet Company" included the ships builders as shareholders. The company was soon known as "Mr Cunard's Company" or, just, "Cunards". The first of his steamers to reach Halifax from Liverpool arrived in 1840 after only twelve and a half days at sea. Eight years later, the service was opened directly to New York.

Samuel Cunard eventually settled in England and as a result of his contribution to the Crimean War effort was knighted in 1859. He died 6 years later, the same year Abraham Lincoln was assassinated.

ELDER DEMPSTER COMPANY

Although trade with West Africa initially concentrated on the profitable business of slave trading, it was the availability of other produce, particularly vegetable oils, which was primarily responsible for its growth in importance to the European markets.

The African Steam Ship Company founded by Royal Charter in 1852 was the first shipping company to establish regular links with the region. Its prime objective was to carry mail for the British Government, for which it was amply rewarded. Capital stock of 11,008 partly-paid shares of £20 each were issued. The Managing Director was MacGregor Laird.

Laird's father founded the shipbuilding company later to become 'Cammell Laird & Co.', while his mother was the daughter of our old friend Gregor Macgregor of Poyais! In its first year the company made a profit of £3,486 but following Laird's death the board erred on the side of caution and this led to the formation of a more aggressive competitor — the British and African Steam Navigation Co.

Two ex-employees of the African Steamship Co. were appointed agents for the new line, their names were John Dempster and Alexander Elder. The Elder Dempster Co. was thus formed in 1868. Sixteen years later the founders retired and their senior clerk, Alfred Jones, took control. Jones was eventually able to act as agent for both shipping groups and thus pulled together the whole West African trade.

Companhia de Navegação. Shares are rarely more elaborate than this one issued in Portugal in 1920.

Not only did the White Star Line come under the control of Lord Kylsant, it also owned the Titanic.

Charles Pratt & Co. A major oil refiner and manufacturer of oil by-products, the company was acquired by Standard Oil. The share shown is issued to Henry H. Rogers, who together with Charles Pratt became two of Standard Oil's guiding spirits.

On Jones's death, the Lords Kylsant and Pirie (the former a director of the Royal Mail Steam Packet Co. and the latter chairman of Harland and Wolff) bought Elder Dempster from the executor for £500,000 through the establishment of Elder Dempster and Company Limited in 1910..

Having merged the lines of Elder Dempster and the Royal Mail Steam Packet Co., Lord Kylsant set out on a process of acquisition, which eventually included sizeable stakes in Lamport & Holt, the Union Castle Steamship Co. and the White Star Line (owner of the Titanic).

All did not go well for Kylsant and, following depressed trade, a management disagreement and rumours of insolvency, the group collapsed in 1931. The first to go was Lamport & Holt. while Kylsant was convicted of giving false information in a prospectus. Following a complex restructuring, the company was reconstituted in 1936 under the name 'Elder Dempster Lines Holdings Ltd.', which is now part of Ocean Transport and Trading Ltd.

Other countries where shipping has played an important part are the United States, Scandinavia and Greece. In the case of the former the shipping companies involved in the Confederate 'Blockade' make a fascinating historical theme.

SOME OTHER THEMES

OIL

Reference has already been made to the Standard Oil Company on page 112, and the subject is clearly a very topical one, but mineral oil (as opposed to vegetable oil) is not only a recent phenomenon. Discoveries, and the resultant oil companies, date from the mid-nineteenth century and although most were small companies from the United States and Canada several other countries such as Russia, Nigeria and Mexico, are also able to boast of relatively early involvement, as demonstrated by the number of share certificates.

Forerunner of Getty Oil, shares in the Mission Development Company carry the facsimile signature of John Paul Getty.

Louisville Bridge Company, showing bridge crossing the Mississippi complete with side wheelers and portraits of the company's founders.

ENTERTAINMENT

The world of entertainment is a broad one and any collector choosing this field must be clear on his horizons. Stretching from hotels through casinos, theatres, cinemas and clubs, the subject can be both amusing and exasperating in its sheer size.

CANALS

Throughout the various thematic chapters, canals has been a subject regularly raised, but often as very much a second string to railways. This is a little unfair as canal certificates are both numerous and intriguing with many dating from the late eighteenth century, indeed canals themselves have been constructed since 3000 BC.

In Britain it was the opening of the Bridgewater Canal in 1761 which initiated the construction boom. This came to a head during the 1790s and continued until about 1830 when competition from railways made such projects less profitable. In America the first two canal companies (Western Inland Navigation Co and the Northern Inland Navigation Company) were formed in 1792 and their surviving shares are some of the earliest American pieces to be found. Activity continued apace throughout Europe greatly encouraged by Napoleon who saw this means of communication as one which not only aided military efficiency but also created national and international unity. Major canals were built in France, Prussia, Spain and Russia at the end of the eighteenth century.

Canals take various forms and whereas early projects were concerned with the creation of inland waterways, later works concentrated on improving shipping. Two of the most famous such developments were the Panama and Suez.

A share in the Corinth Canal Company from 1882 which includes both a map of the area and a cross section of the land mass.

The Suez and Panama Canals

A renewed upsurge of interest in canals which occurred during the latter half of the nineteenth century was almost wholly due to Ferdinand de Lesseps and his success in constructing the Suez Canal. The idea of a shipping route across the desert was one originally formulated by Napoleon but it was the perseverance of De Lesseps which saw that dream fulfilled.

De Lesseps' friendship with the Egyptian Royal Family enabled him to obtain a licence to construct the canal and work began in 1854 and was completed in 1869. Opened by the Empress Eugenie of France, the result was viewed by the French as a national triumph rivalling Britain's earlier superiority in railways. Following a period of financial losses, Egypt's interest in the canal was acquired by Britain and remained that way until it was forcibly nationalised by Nasser in 1956, 12 years before legal ownership was due to be transferred to Egypt under de Lesseps' original agreement.

Bonds and shares of the Suez Canal company are surprisingly rare and generally well sought after. Shares in the Panama Canal are, however, easier to obtain probably due to the vast numbers issued.

De Lesseps' success in Egypt convinced him that his name alone would be sufficient to ensure successful construction of a similar venture across the Central American isthmus. This was not to be.

Prior to work starting on the Panama Canal there had been numerous ideas and ventures formulated to cut out the lengthy sea voyage around Cape Horn. Some, such as Rockefeller's Accessory Transit Company proved reasonably successful in making use of rivers, lakes and roads whereas others such as the British Honduras Company which promoted the concept of transporting ships on trains overland, never got off the ground.

The "Compagnie Universelle du Canal Inter-Oceanique de Panama" was incorporated in 1881.

Capital was initially raised by shares but the first issue was not a success and subsequent issues were only achieved with the help of favourable press comment and sizeable bribes. Construction proved difficult and by 1889 the company crashed with the work far from finished, despite the company having raised 1.3 billion Francs in shares, bonds and lottery issues. An investigation turned up all kinds of bad practices and implicated many politicians and well known figures. De Lesseps and his son were arrested and each sentenced to 5 years imprisonment. There are several types of shares available to the collector, most bearing the facsimile signature of de Lesseps.

Completion of the Panama Canal was left to the Americans with the first ship passing through in 1914.

De Lesseps' success with Suez had also encouraged construction of yet another famous canal, this time at Corinth. Work began in 1882 but the collapse of the Panama Canal Company in 1889 also caused the downfall of the "Canal Maritime de Corinthe" which was subsequently acquired by a Greek company and eventually opened by the King of Greece in 1893.

HERALDRY

A great many bonds and shares carry heraldic devices, usually with the intention of adding credibility to their financial objectives. Some, such as the Russian City bonds, are correctly displayed, whereas others, such as those of Poyais, are a mere fabrication designed to impress. There are many stringent rules governing the portrayal of coats of arms and an incorrect display is often indicative of a shady concern. The collector of this theme must combine the knowledge of two hobbies in order to maximise his benefit, but the end result can be most interesting.

OTHERS

It is not intended that the following list should be taken as comprehensive and indeed permutations could considerably add to the overall number of options; nevertheless, the list might provoke some thoughts:

Agriculture	Food	Movies	Telephones
Aeroplanes	Glass	Munitions	Textiles
Animals	Horses	Music & Art	Theatres
Buildings	Insurance	Photography	Tea
Cemeteries	Land	Publishing	Tobacco
Clasped Hands	Libraries	Radio	Toys
Coal	Lighting	Retail Sales	Trade Associations
Events	Lumber	Rubber	Tramways
Exhibitions	Medical	Sports	Water
Fish & Fishing	Metals & Iron	Sugar	Wine

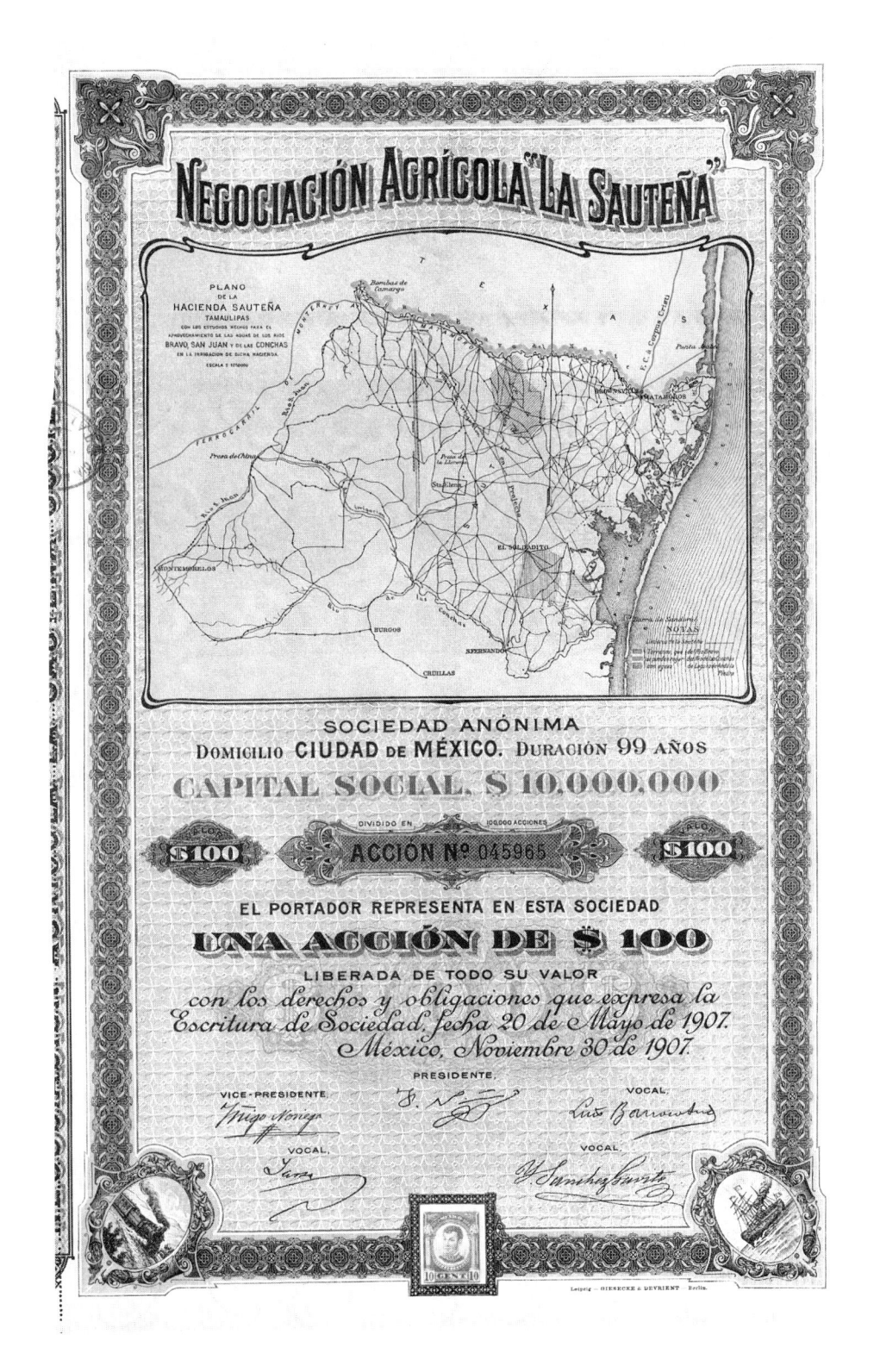

Maps on bonds and shares are a popular collecting theme. The Mexican Negociación Agrícola "La Sauteña" is an excellent example depicting the land owned by the hacienda.

PART 3

Developing a collection

WHAT TO LOOK FOR AND WHAT TO AVOID

Part 2 provided a wide selection of themes on which to base a collection. This chapter considers the major features of bonds and shares which assist in determining relative value. There are five determinants of value:
1. Condition
2. Rarity
3. Age and historical significance
4. Signature
5. Attractiveness

In view of their significance, each will be covered in some detail. Their order implies no ranking in importance.

1. CONDITION

To appreciate the meaning of "condition" it is important to bear in mind the very nature of bonds and shares. These were not printed with the collector in mind, they were printed to be used and those issued to bearer have undergone considerable handling during their active life. At each transaction they were sorted and passed between offices; their large size will have necessitated folding and changing interest rates may have involved the attachment of new coupon sheets in place of the old. Smaller issues and higher denomination bonds may have changed hands more frequently, it being far easier for a broker to count two £1,000 bonds than twenty £100 bonds.

Whitehead Aircraft was one of the earliest manufacturers of planes and this is a classic and well sought after share dated 1918. Signed by the two founders Jack and Digby Whitehead.

Registered material, as opposed to bearer, is also likely to have suffered through handling. Sold shares may well have found their way back to the company registrar who, in some cases of extreme diligence went to the trouble of matching the share to its original "stub" and worse still, actually glued them together! Others may have been nastily cancelled with heavy ink lines or "bullet holes".

It is important when looking at condition to bear the above in mind and it is almost essential to determine condition relative to the issue itself. Below average condition should never be the sole reason for declining an item; it is quite possible that certain issues will always only be found in poor condition, for various reasons, such as poor quality paper, the small size of the loan itself, age or even the physical size of the certificates.

The decision of whether or not to purchase an item of dubious condition must take full account of these factors in the context of the overall collection. It is often better to purchase what is offered (at a favourable price) and at a later date trade in the item for a better piece when available.

The following provides examples of bonds and shares which are often of below-average condition.

ISSUE	REASON FOR CONDITION
Chinese 1918 Marconi	Poor paper. Small issue.
City of Moscow 1908, £500	High denomination. Well traded.
City of Riga 1913	Almost wholly repaid; those still around have had considerable battering from man and mouse.
Russian 1822 Rothschild	Soft paper. Early date.
Confederate Bonds	Early date. Printed on poor paper.
Pre-1840 US Rail shares	Age and heavy cancellation marks.

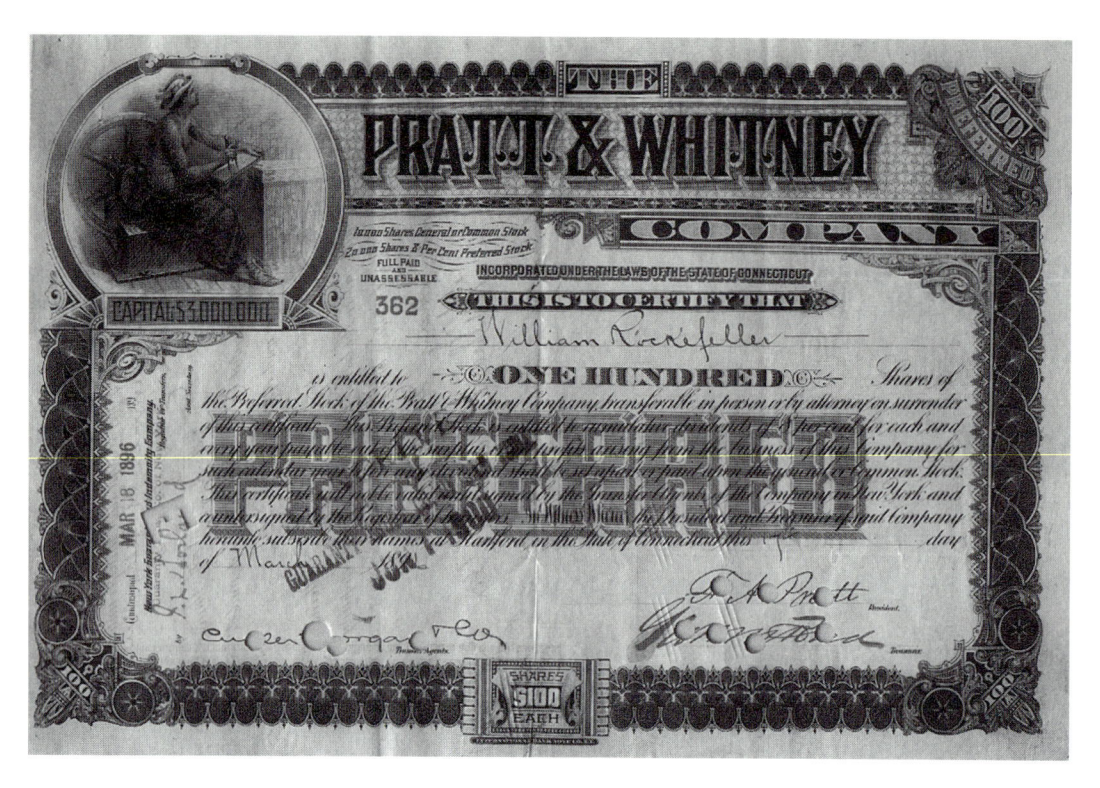

Organized in 1860, Pratt & Whitney was a pioneer in the manufacture of machine tools for the sewing machine and armaments industries. The share illustrated is signed by Pratt and issued to William Rockefeller (brother of John D.).

At the other extreme is unissued material. Many collectors shy away from unissued shares and bonds; the lack of signatures, embossed company seals, revenue stamps and dirty thumb prints somehow give a feeling of unreality, but in point of fact it is usually unissued material which is rarer than the issued. Unissued certificates were held as reserve stock to cover the registration of new shareholders or the replacement of lost certificates. To be technically correct, those certificates with a serial number are simply 'unissued', and those without are usually 'reserve stock' — the latter kept for issue as 'duplicates' and therefore able to be given the same number as the original. Specimens (see page 22) also fall into this category and most are in EF condition although it is sometimes interesting to find specimens which bear inked corrections and instructions to the printer.

Bearing in mind earlier comments, and as a general guide only, the following grades are those usually used by dealers and auction houses together with an indication of the kind of price differences which may arise:

DESCRIPTION	CONDITION	PRICE INDEX
EF (Extremely Fine)	some minor folds, clean, almost as issued	100
VF (Very Fine)	some folds and creases, slight wear	85-90
F (Fine)	circulated and worn, but very slight damage	50-55
P (Poor)	much used, some damage	10-20

"G" preceding a grade indicates a condition slightly better (for example, GVF is rather better than

Plans to build a Channel Tunnel connecting England with France were well in hand over 100 years ago as this share testifies. The first Channel Tunnel Railway company was founded in 1892. The Tunnel was finally opened in 1994.

VF but not as good as EF), whilst "A" preceding a grade indicates a condition slightly worse (for example, AVF means not quite as good as VF).

Inevitably such a system of grading is subjective and where possible any prospective purchaser is always advised to inspect first, particularly when buying at auction.

2. RARITY

Four factors create rarity: high demand, low initial issue, a high level of redemption (in the case of bonds) and age.

A certificate which falls into only one of the above categories, although rare, may well not carry a high value. Most quality pieces have at least two of the above attributes. The Standard Oil certificate, for example, not only bears a famous signature, but is also dated 1875 and believed to be limited to 275-325 pieces. At the other extreme is the Russian 1894 3 1/2% Gold Loan, 2nd issue, Frs. 12,500, of which only six bonds were issued — interest in Russian State bonds is still in its infancy and consequently such an item will not, at this stage, command a high price.

It is, therefore, unwise to buy solely for scarcity reasons. High demand is essential if the main objective is capital appreciation and, remember also, the rarer a piece the smaller will be the market in that item and unless seen from time to time at auction its very existence may be forgotten. This latter point is also important in determining your collecting theme. Unless highly determined (and wealthy) it can be discouraging to choose a sector of such scarcity that its constituents rarely appear. But, having said this, nearly all sectors contain certain items which are rare, and chasing these — at the right price — can prove to be the most satisfying part of building a collection.

Rarity must always be balanced with condition and demand, and never taken in isolation as a determinant of value.

3. AGE & HISTORICAL SIGNIFICANCE

In the case of registered share certificates, age is, without doubt, a major determinant of value, adding both historical interest and the likelihood of fewer certificates having survived the ravages of time.

Material which pre-dates 1820 may be considered very early, and pre-1800, both extremely early and rare. Depending on your chosen collecting theme, age may or may not be relevant. Chinese bonds, for example, all date between 1896 and 1937, whereas those who collect Confederate Bonds are, by definition, all seeking material issued in the 1860s'. Set against the advantage of history, however, one must always consider condition, and a badly torn certificate of almost any age is seldom of much value. Although professional repairs can produce a transformation, at time of sale it should always be clearly stated if a bond or certificate has been repaired.

4. SIGNATURES

This feature has been largely covered in the earlier section on collecting themes, but it is worth emphasizing the value of famous signatures. Without exhaustive historical knowledge it is very easy to overlook a signature. Remember, share certificates are often signed on both front and back, and it is always worth checking names carefully. A well-known figure in South African history may be unknown to a collector of US Railroads and vice-versa. A famous signature can increase the value by up to ten times, which makes careful scrutiny and research well worthwhile.

5. ATTRACTIVENESS

Certainly not a crucial factor in the setting of value, attractiveness nevertheless contributes greatly to the overall interest and appeal of a certificate. But a word of warning; do not pay high prices purely on the strength of beauty. If the item is new to you, check the number issued. This may be stated on the certificate itself but if not, a good clue can be obtained from the serial number — 210,642 means precisely what you think it means — your certificate is not unique.

The five value determinants of condition, rarity, age, signature and attractiveness are all key factors to consider when adding a new piece to your collection. This chapter has stressed the importance of not being too influenced by any one feature — always consider certificates in their particular context and make your assessment accordingly.

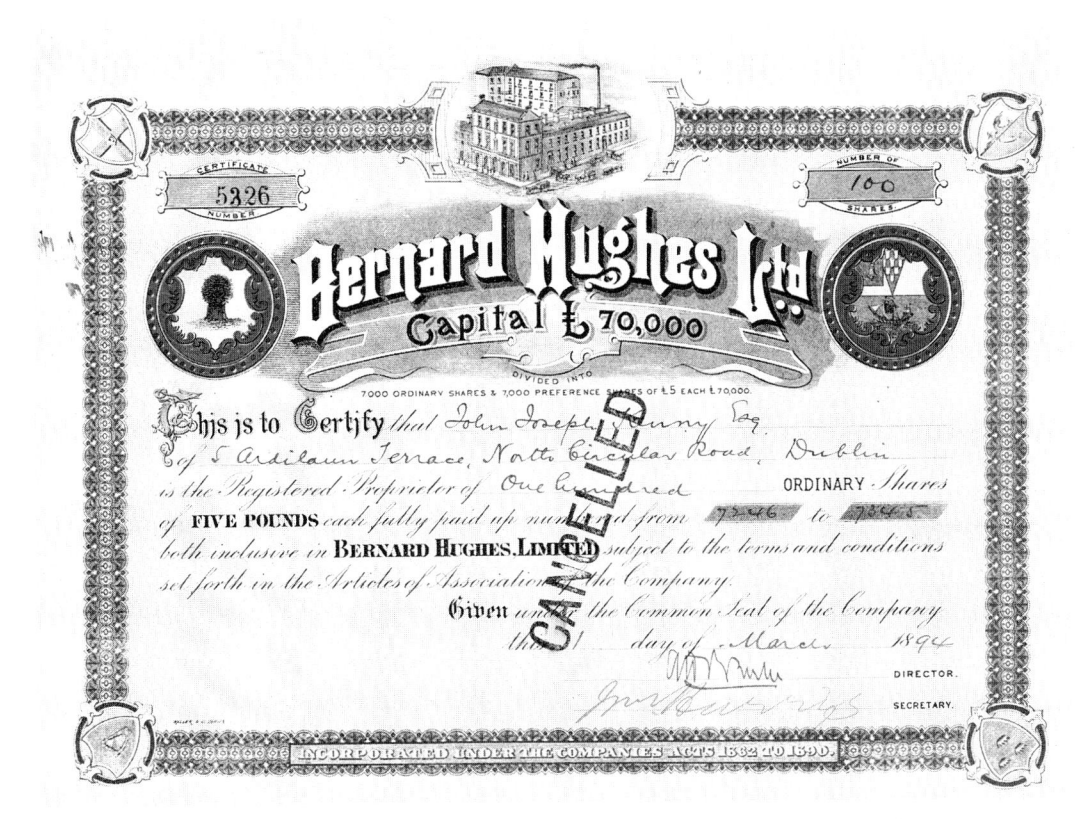

To those living in Belfast during the early part of this century the name "Barny Hughes" was synonymous with bread. Bernard Hughes Ltd. dominated the market and its share certificates are unusually decorative and colourful for British material.

LOOKING AFTER A COLLECTION

Having spent a great deal of time selecting your theme and acquiring the first few pieces, it would be unfortunate to allow lethargy to take hold, for now is the time when you can really get to grips with the business of collecting.

First step — get it insured. The danger is not so much from the local burglar, who probably has never seen a certificate before, but from the godly elements of fire and water. Most insurance companies are prepared to add the value of a collection, whatever its field, to a normal household policy, unless there are individual items of particularly high value, in which case a listing may be required. An official valuation may be requested but, if your original purchase invoices do not suffice, most dealers will provide a valuation, probably for a small charge.

Financial protection does not end with insurance, however, and it is important to realise that bad storage can lead to a steady process of deterioration. Often this is not discovered until you decide to sell and a dealer points out newly scuffed edges, green mould, fresh mouse holes, or worse.

STORAGE

Unless you are one of those who keep everything in a bank vault or framed on your walls, you will probably store your certificates at home and gain pleasure from seeing them from time to time. The sheer size of some bonds causes problems for even the most dedicated, but do try not to bend them. There are three main rules that should be followed: always lay certificates flat, keep them dry and fully enclose them in an album or other container.

Most large-format bonds and shares will, almost certainly, have spent a significant part of their life folded, thus causing damage to the paper. Halt the deterioration by opening them out and enclose in a protective cover, preferably acid-free, or as near to it as possible. Most albums and sheets sold by reputable dealers are adequate. If you live in a humid environment allow air to circulate among the collection and avoid piling plastic sheets on top of one another.

REPAIR AND CLEANING

Like any kind of restoration work, 'paper conservation' is a highly-skilled craft. Professional repairs take time and cost money. Damage takes various forms, most of which can be halted or even rectified. Main causes and remedies are listed below:

1. Dirt and stains. Caused by constant handling or being left in dusty areas. Yellowing may result from sulphuric acid in the atmosphere and other stains from ink, for example. Most stains can be removed by dry cleaning and washing, but take care with blue ink — it runs! Solvents or bleaching may be used for persistent marks, but such treatment is better carried out by a professional.
2. Unsuitable backings. Certificates may have been pasted into share registers or on to board. These can be removed completely and if the piece is very fragile it can be strengthened with a backing of thin Japanese tissue.
3. Tears and damaged edges. Usually caused by excessive handling, these can be professionally knitted together and backed by thin tissue.
4. Creases. Large bonds have often been folded, thus weakening the paper and causing splits and tears. Creases can be eased out and pressed and weakened areas may be strengthened.
5. Missing corners and holes. The crispness of the paper ('sizing') may have been knocked out as a result of age and handling, leaving the paper limp and easily liable to tear. Sizing can be restored by brushing a size of leaf gelatine on to the back of the certificate.

Many bonds and shares have experienced an obviously hard life, and it is often the most rare which incurred greatest damage. Expert repair work, although costly, can enhance the value of an item, but do-it-yourself jobs may prove disastrous. A repaired item will never have the same value as an EF or VF piece and it should always be described as having undergone repair when listed in dealers' or auctioneers' catalogues.

A tip for those minor clean-up jobs — it is amazing what can be achieved with a soft eraser lightly applied across the whole certificate. And, for the launderette enthusiast, most shares can be relieved of their backing paper by a twenty minute soak in the bath, but watch for running signatures (black ink is usually waterproof). Iron from the back through a piece of heavy paper to avoid scorching and shining. Experiments should be limited to less expensive items and is really only recommended for the very careful and dextrous amateur. Under no circumstances should vellum be ironed — it shrivels up!

The Sudan Land & Commercial Company. £5 share issued in Alexandria in 1909.

FRAMING

There are few of us with either the wall space or the desire to frame a whole collection, but the attractiveness and size of bonds make them ideal candidates for putting behind glass, and one or two well-placed pieces can add considerable character and colour to a home or office.

There are few rules to remember about framing, but nevertheless they are very important. Stress to your framer that acid-free backing materials must be used and quite definitely, no glue or scotch tape! Whether you choose normal or non-reflecting glass is a matter of personal taste, but avoid hanging in direct sunlight.

CATALOGUING AND RESEARCH

Keep a careful register of your collection, note prices paid and dates purchased, and record auction and dealer prices. Such data will prove useful should you choose to sell at some future date, providing a good guide to value. The method and sophistication of cataloguing adopted is very much up to personal choice ranging from a personal computer to the back of an envelope. Whatever your approach, a complete set of records will aid your knowledge and interest in developing a collection.

Compared with more developed collecting fields, such as stamps and coins, relatively little published material exists on scripophily. The opportunity for personal research is enormous and can prove to be a fascinating and rewarding experience. Many have a secret ambition to put pen to paper and here is a perfect opportunity. Magazines are always seeking new articles and a well-researched and written piece has every chance of achieving publication. Even if literary fame is not your ambition, researching a collection not only gives pleasure but also adds value.

HOW AND WHERE TO SELL

Building up a collection can be a long, slow and, hopefully, enjoyable process. At the time, thoughts of selling may well be far from your mind, but the ability to be able to sell at some future date is always reassuring, particularly when debating whether or not to purchase more expensive pieces. Many collectors consider the act of selling to be a fundamental part of collecting, effectively becoming mini dealers — frequently buying, selling and exchanging items. Active trade between collectors indicates a strong market, and arises for two main reasons: increasing specialisation (refining a collection makes non-compatible items redundant), and, profit (acquiring a quantity of certificates may well present the purchaser with the chance of covering the cost of one piece by selling the rest).

As with all collecting hobbies, a balance between time and price exists and the following rules have as much application to fine paintings as to bonds and shares:
- Do not expect to make money or even fully recover your initial outlay by selling within a few years of purchase.
- Selling in a hurry will always prove disadvantageous. Take a month or so to check out all possibilities.

But before selling, attempt to develop a range of expected values.

PUTTING A VALUE ON YOUR COLLECTION

The first chapter of Part 3 dealt with the major determinants of value: condition, rarity, age, signature and attractiveness. The comments made will help you determine the value of your collection for re-sale purposes. Without the assistance of an expert it is perhaps difficult to objectively assess the true quality of your collection, nevertheless it is not difficult to come close to the truth.

Determining resale value based on original cost can be misleading. If your initial purchases were of poor quality and low value, you can rest assured that when you come to sell, nothing will have changed! If, on the other hand your purchases were of average to good quality or better, then there is

The Yarmouth Aquarium Society Ltd. Unusual English share from 1877.

no doubt that resale is possible and the amount you are able to get will depend on three factors, the current demand, the state of the economy and the length of time you have held the collection.

The first two points are self explanatory but the third needs a little comment.

It is unrealistic to expect to be able to recover the original outlay on a collection for at least three years. Dealer margins and sales taxes must first be exceeded and these, on average items, may amount to around 40% of the retail price. It should be remembered that margins on good quality items are less but margins on cheap and common items are usually more.

In order to arrive at a sensible value, it is necessary to approach the matter from several directions and having arrived at several answers, make a reasonable assessment. The following are suggested:
1. Check current dealer price lists, cost up the collection and reduce the total by 40%.
2. Take your original cost and increase it by 5% per year for every year after year 3.
3. Ask more than one dealer how much he would pay you for it.

This kind of arbitrary approach assumes an average collection and can only be used as a guide. You may well have acquired particularly rare pieces and these will almost certainly appreciate more quickly than others. Such items should be individually valued by dealers and auctioneers.

Remember, however, no matter how a figure is arrived at mathematically, in the final analysis value is what someone is prepared to pay. So who are these potential buyers?

AUCTIONS AND DEALERS

Buying or selling at auction introduces an air of excitement which many find irresistible. The two contrary beliefs that it is both cheaper to buy at auction and also more profitable to sell there, have resulted in the establishment of frequent auctions across the world.

Bidding at auction can indeed be an exciting experience, but remember it is easy to get carried away and pay too high a price; remember also that the buyer is responsible for ascertaining the quality of the goods offered for sale, a caveat which most auction houses clearly state in their conditions. A buyer should never bid blind and although the standard classifications of EF, VF, etc. may be provided these are nothing more than a guide.

Auction houses employ specialists who are able to provide prospective sellers with estimates of prices likely to be achieved. Such advice is usually given free of charge and once you have gained an initial personal 'feel' of the value of your collection, a visit to an auctioneer is no bad thing. Auction houses make their money on commissions which are usually only earned if a lot is sold; the more lots they are able to sell an hour, the higher their overall income. Thus, they are not interested in offering pieces which they consider to be overpriced or of no interest. It is also quite usual to impose a minimum value per lot, thus, there is little point in trying to sell a low value item at auction — it will either not be accepted in the first place or the minimum fixed commission will account for most of the expected price. Only selected pieces should be auctioned. These pieces should be the unusual or rarer items which could well realize considerably more at auction than by selling to a dealer.

Care should be taken in choosing which auction houses to use and in which country. There is little point in auctioning early German material in the USA as the market for that field lies in Germany and that is where it will achieve best prices. Certain houses are better for buying than selling and before consigning material for sale, a little research on the subject is advised.

Guidelines for selling at auction are as follows:
1. Get a feel for the value of particular items to help determine your reserve price.
2. Select the right material for auction; preferably the unusual or rare.
3. Select the right auction house in the right country.
4. Check on any commissions payable by you as a seller.

After an initial visit to the auctioneer and before committing anything for sale through that medium, call on your dealer — and not just one dealer, but as many as you have time to visit, and the emphasis is on VISIT. Standard letters through the mail, with or without photocopies, are insufficient. If you want a quick decision a dealer needs to see the actual items for sale in order to check condition and your physical presence will prompt a fast response, whereas letters can easily be left on one side.

There are several options open to a dealer and he or she may well suggest a combination of methods of disposal so as to maximize your return. The most obvious is to buy outright and, although this may not provide you with the highest price, it does have the benefit of immediacy and simplicity. An alternative would be to sell on commission; your bonds would be offered to clients and, on completion of a sale, the proceeds less commission would be paid to you. Commission rates vary among dealers, but fifteen to twenty per cent is about the norm. Another alternative is for the dealer to put the material into auction for you, being more aware of forthcoming auctions throughout the world and better placed than the private collector to select the most appropriate. Once again you should expect to pay a fee for this service (5-10%).

A good dealer should always be able to come up with a programme of disposal. But if dealers and auction house are not for you, there is always another alternative.

Akcionarsky Pivovar na Smichove. One of Czechoslovakia's early Pils brewing companies. The buildings shown still exist today, but probably not the King enjoying his beer!

Baumwoll-Spinnerei Kolbermoor. Bavarian company typical of many which were formed to develop the textile industry in the early days of industrialisation. The company still exists but is now involved in real estate.

PRIVATE SALE

Successful private sale can often result in achievement of the best prices, but it takes time, patience and, where advertising is involved, money. Apart from selling to friends and acquaintances, your options are to advertise or send lists of available items to known collectors.

Lists of known collectors are usually available from your local society — a further reason for joining. Not much else can be added about private sale except to say that it is possibly the hardest way of disposing of a collection.

THE LAST WORD

If you have reached this point, it can only be assumed that the subject has generated some interest. This book is not intended as an A-Z of scripophily, merely an introduction with the inclusion of a little history designed to whet the appetite.

No Swedish student of finance can claim not to have heard of Kreuger & Toll. The company once dominated the world match business and became powerful enough to lend to several European Governments. Accusations of fraud finished the company and Ivar Kreuger commited suicide.

Having come so far you may now wish to start or build on a collection and with this in mind the Appendices which follow are intended to assist. Dealers, auction houses, publications and Societies are all listed and hopefully, armed with such information, you will now be ready to become a true "scripophilist"! May it give you as much pleasure as it has given me.

APPENDICES

MAJOR DEALERS, AUCTION HOUSES, PUBLICATIONS AND SOCIETIES

DEALERS

Belgium
Centrum voor Scriptophilie,
Kouter 126, B-9800 DEINZE, Belgium.
Contact: Erik Boone
Telephone: 93-86-90-91
Fax: 93-86-97-66

Canada
Canadian Antique Paper Research Associates,
6 Regency Court,
Oakville, ONTARIO L6H 2P7 Canada.
Contact: Geoff Cole/
Nancy McKenna
Telephone: 905-845-2860
Fax: 905-338-0498

Germany
Aktien-Galerie GmbH,
Spetzgarter Weg 1, D-88662 UBERLINGEN, Germany.
Telephone: 07551-1335
Fax: 07551-65680

Benecke & Rehse
Wertpapierantiquariat GmbH,
Am Hogrevenkamp 4, D-38302 WOLFENBUTTEL, Germany.
Contact: Michael Rösler
Telephone: 05331-72890
Fax: 05331-31575

Classic Effecten GmbH,
P.O.B. 4066, D-47730 KREFELD, Germany.
Contact: Rudiger K. Weng
Telephone: 2151-500 (400)

Historic Papers,
Bahnstrasse 10, D-50181 BEDBURG, Germany.
Contact: Marianne Schmidt
Telephone/Fax: 2272-81390

Wertpapier-Antiquariat,
Schaedestrasse 7, Postfach 370426,
D-14134, BERLIN, Germany.
Contact: Stefan Adam
Telephone: 30 8158465
Fax: 30 8153641

South Africa
Collectable Books,
The Village, 60 Tyrone Ave., Parkview,
Johannesburg, 2193, South Africa.
Contact: Michael Prior
Telephone: (011) 646-8320
Fax: (011) 486-2864

Sweden
Cafmeyer
Box 5235
S - 31205 SKOTTORP Sweden
Telephone: (46) 430 20406
Fax: (46) 430 21405

Switzerland
Sharecol AG,
Hafenstrasse 50 A,CH-8280 KREUZLINGEN, Switzerland.

Galerie Sevogel AG,
Sevogelstrasse 76, CH-4052 BASEL, Switzerland.
Contact: T. Stäuble
Telephone: 061-3122659
Fax: 061-3123551

Anciens titres Galerie du Rhône,
Ch. des Peupliers 15, 3960 SIERRE, Switzerland.
Contact: M. Husi
Telephone: 027 55 36 23
Fax: 027 55 36 23

United Kingdom
G. K. R. Bonds Ltd.,
Unit 4, Park Farm, Inworth,
COLCHESTER, Essex CO5 9SH, England.
Contact: Hazel Fisher
or Geoff Metzger
Telephone: 01376 571711
Fax: 01376 570125

Herzog Hollender Phillips & Co.
(THE SCRIPOPHILY SHOP),
Britannia Hotel, Grosvenor Square,
LONDON W1A 3AN, England.
Contact: Keith Hollender
Telephone: 0171-495 0580
Fax: 0171-495 0565

M. Veissid & Co.,
6/7 Castle Gates, SHREWSBURY,
Shropshire SY1 2AE, England.
Contact: Michael Veissid
Telephone: 01743 272140
Fax: 01743 366041

Scripophily International Promotions,
Room 645, Linen Hall, 162-168 Regent Street, LONDON W1R 5TV, England.
Contact: Leslie Tripp
Telephone/Fax: 0171-437 4588

U.S.A.
American Vignettes,
P.O. Box 155, ROSELLE PARK,
NJ 07204, USA.
Contact: Bob Kluge
Telephone/Fax: 908-241-4209

Antique Securities
11145 Lake Chapel Lane, RESTON,
VA 22091, USA.
Contact: Richard W. Malone
Telephone: 703 620-1667
and 703 827-7628

Antique Stocks & Bonds,
Drawer JH, WILLIAMSBURG,
VA 23187-3632, USA.
Contact: Haley Garrison
Telephone: 804-220-3838/
800-451-4504
Fax: 804-220-0294

David M. Beach,
P.O. Box 2026, GOLDENROD,
FL 32733, USA.
Telephone: 407-657-7403
Fax: 407-657-6382

Colonel Grover Criswell,
15001 N. E. 248th Ave. Rd., SALT SPRINGS, FL 32134-6000, USA.
Telephone: 904-685-2287
Fax: 904-685-2358

Clinton Hollins,
P.O. Box 112, SPRINGFIELD,
VA 22150, USA.
Telephone: 703-644-0933

Investment Research Institute,
3043 Clayton Road, CONCORD,
CA 94519-2730, USA.
Contact: Fred Fuld III
Telephone/Fax: 510-686-9067

George H. LaBarre Galleries,
P.O.Box 746, Hollis, NEW HAMPSHIRE 03049, USA.
Contact: George LaBarre
Telephone: 603-882-2411
Fax: 603-882-4797

Ken Prag Paper Americana,
Box 531, BURLINGAME, CA 94011, USA.
Contact: Ken Prag
Telephone: 415-566-6400

R. M. Smythe & Co., Inc.,
26 Broadway Suite 271, NEW YORK,
NY 10004-1701, USA.
Contact: Steve Goldsmith/
Diana Herzog
Telephone: 212-943-1880/
800-622-1880
Fax: 212-908-4047

Stock Search International Inc.,
10855 N. Glen Abbey Dr., TUCSON,
AZ 85737, USA.
Contact: Micheline Massé
Telephone: 602-544-2590/
800-537-4523
Fax: 602 544-9395

Scott J. Winslow Associates Inc.
P.O. Box 10240, BEDFORD, NH 03110,
USA.
Contact: Scott J. Winslow
Telephone: 603-472-7040
Fax: 603-472-8773

AUCTION HOUSES

Antik Effekten GmbH,
Westendstrasse 79, D- 60325
FRANKFURT, Germany.
Contact: Michael Steinke
Telephone: 069 751183
Fax: 069 751185

Auktionhaus Rheinhild Tschöpe,
Bruchweg 8, D-41564, Kaarst,
Germany.
Contact: Rheinhild Tschöpe
Telephone: (02131) 602756
Fax: (02131) 667949

Freunde Historischer Wertpapiere
Auktionsges,
Am Hogrevenkamp 4, D-38302,
WOLFENBUTTEL, Germany.
Contact: Jörg Benecke
Telephone: (49) 5331 72890
Fax: (49) 5331 31575

Galerie Sevogel AG,
Sevogelstrasse 76, CH - 4052 BASEL,
Switzerland.
Contact: T. Staüble
Telephone: 061-3122659
Fax: 061-3123551

H. J. W. Daugherty,
P.O. Box 1146 F, EASTHAM,
Mass. 02642, USA.
Contact: Hugh Daugherty
Telephone: 508-255-7488

R. M. Smythe & Co., Inc.,
26 Broadway Suite 271, NEW YORK,
NY 10004, USA.
Contact: Steve Goldsmith/
Diana Herzog
Telephone: 212-943-1880/
800-622-1880
Fax: 212-908-4047

Sotheby's,
34 New Bond Street,
London W1A 2AA, England.
Contact: Tim Robson
Telephone: 0171-493 8080

George H. LaBarre Galleries,
P.O.Box 746, Hollis, NEW HAMPSHIRE
03049, USA.
Contact: George LaBarre
Telephone: 603-882-2411
Fax: 603-882-4797

Centrum voor Scriptophilie,
Kouter 126, B-9800 DEINZE, Belgium.
Contact: Erik Boone
Telephone: 93-86-90-91
Fax: 93-86-97-66

Scott J. Winslow Associates Inc.
P.O. Box 10240, BEDFORD, NH 03110,
USA.
Contact: Scott J. Winslow
Telephone: 603-472-7040
Fax: 603-472-8773

PUBLICATIONS (other than those issued by the Collectors' Clubs and Societies)

Bond & Share — Der
Wertpapiersammler,
Spetzgarter Weg 1, 88662
UBERLINGEN, Germany.
Telephone: 07551-69133
Fax: 07551-65680

Friends of Financial History,
26 Broadway Room 200, NEW YORK,
NY 10004, USA.
Contact: Diane Moore
Telephone: 212-908-4519
Fax: 212-908-4600

ORGANISATIONS

Museum of American Financial
History,
26 Broadway, Room 200, NEW YORK,
NY 10004, USA.
Contact: Diane Moore
Telephone: 212-908-4519
Fax: 212-908-4600

COLLECTORS' CLUBS AND SOCIETIES

Belgium
Association Belge de Scriptophilie
(Vereniging voor Scriptophilie),
107 av. de Cheremont, 1300 WAVRE,
Belgium.
Contact: Jean-Pierre Magos

Canada
Canadian Bond & Share Society
80 Churchill Avenue, North York,
ONTARIO M2N 1Y9, Canada.
Contact: Raymond Schaffer

France
Association Francaise des
Collectionneurs de Titres Anciens,
55 rue Rennequin, 75017 Paris, France.

Germany
EDHAC,
Weingartnerstrasse 26, D-76229
KARLSRUHE, Germany.
Contact: Prof. Wanner

Deutsche Geldschein-und
Wertpapiersammler,
Myliusgarten 30, 12587 BERLIN-
FRIEDRICHSHAGEN, Germany.
Contact: Heinz-Wilhelm Thiede

Italy
Conservatoria Titoli Storici,
Via Ausonia 6, 20123 MILANO, Italy.
Contact: Sauro Ripamonti

Netherlands
Vereniging van Verzamelaars van
Oude Fondsen,
Postbus 17071, 1001 JB AMSTERDAM,
The Netherlands.
Contact: J. E. Wustenhoff

Norway
Norsk Selskap for Scripofili,
Postboks 48, Ovre Ullern, 0311
OSLO 3, Norway.
Contact: Anders Walle Jensen

Portugal
Associacao Portuguesa de
Coleccionadores de Papeis de Valor,
Av. da Igreja 63C, 1700 LISBOA,
Portugal.

South Africa
South African Bond & Share Society,
P O Box 41292, CRAIGHALL 2024,
South Africa.
Contact: Maria Loudon

Sweden
Svenska Foreningen for Historiska
Vardepapper,
Box 16 246, 103 25 STOCKHOLM,
Sweden.
Contact: Kurt M. Holm

Switzerland
Scripofilia Helvetica,
Latti 361, CH-3053
MUNCHENBUSCHEE, Switzerland.
Contact: Urs Strub

Nonvaleur-Club-Zurich,
Postfach 4568, CH-8022 ZURICH,
Switzerland.

U.K.
International Bond & Share Society,
P.O. Box 9, TADWORTH,
Surrey KT20 7JU, England.
Contact: Brian Mills

U.S.A.
International Bond & Share Society
Drawer JH, WILLIAMSBURG,
VA 23187-3632, USA.
Contact: Haley Garrison

WHACO! (Washington Historical
Autograph & Certificate Organization),
P.O. Box 2428, SPRINGFIELD,
VA 22152-0428, USA.
Contact: George Teas
Telephone/Fax: 703-866-0175

BIBLIOGRAPHY

In order to compile this book a wide variety of reference books have been used. Most are listed below and those which the collector may find of specific benefit have been asterisked.

* * Anderson, William G. *The Price of Liberty,* 1983. (American Revolutionary War Debt Certificates.)
* Arnold, David *Britain, Europe and the World* 1871-1971 Edward Arnold
* Austin, K. A. *The Lights of Cobb & Co.* Angus & Robertson
* Bagwell, Philip S. *The Transport Revolution from 1770* B.T. Batsford Ltd.
* * Ball, Douglas B. *Financial Failure and Confederate Defeat.*
* * Ball, Douglas B. *Register of the Confederate Debt.*
* Boulton, W. H. *The Pageant of Transport Through the Ages* Blom
* * Cifre, G. — *3000 Titre Francais*
  * — *La France en Titre*
  * — *La France d'Outre-Mer*
* Cipolla, Carlo M. the *Fontana Economic History of Europe* 1980
* Clews, Henry. *Twenty Eight Years in Wall Street* 1888
* * Council of Foreign Bondholders, *London Annual Reports*
* * Criswell, Grover C. *Confederate and Southern State Bonds* 1979
* Davies, P. N. *The Trade Makers (Elder Dempster in West Africa 1852-1972)* George Allen & Unwin
* * Dawson, Frank Griffith. *The First Latin American Debt Crisis* Yale University Press 1990
* * Drumm, Henseler & May, Old Securities,   1978 Colour illustrations
* *   ,,   ,,   ,, ,,   ,,   ,,   Chinese Bonds & Shares 1976
*   ,,   ,,   ,, ,,   ,,   ,,   Russian Railway Bonds 1979
*   ,,   ,,   ,, ,,   ,,   ,,   Russian City Bonds 1981
*   ,,   ,,   ,, ,,   ,,   ,,   Austrian Railway Shares and Bonds, 1982
* * Drumm, Henseler & Witula,   Italian Railway Shares and Bonds, 1982
* Drumm, Henseler & Glasemann,   Ottoman Empire & Turkey 1983
* * Edwards, Susan. *Hughesovka — A Welsh Enterprise in Imperial Russia,* Glamorgan Record Office
* * *Encyclopaedia Britannica*
* * *Friends of Financial History Magazine,* Museum of American Financial History, New York
* Frostick, Michael *A History of Motors & Motoring* Vol. 2 Haynes
* * Garrison, G. H. *The Insider's Guide to Antique Securities.*
* Grant, K. Samuel *Cunard Pioneer of the Atlantic Steamship* Abelard Schuman 1967
* Hadfield, Charles *World Canals,* David & Charles 1986
* Hatch, Alder *American Express 1850-1950* Doubleday & Co. Inc. 1950
* *Haydns Dictionary of Dates,* Ward Lock 1898
* * Hendy, A. M. *American Railroad Stock Certificates,* 1980.
* Hessler, E. *Illustrated History of US Loans 1775-1898.*
* Holbrook, Stewart H. *The Age of the Moguls,* Doubleday & Co., 1953
* * *International Bond & Share Society Journals*
* Ingham John N., *Biographical Dictionary of American Business Leaders,* Greenwood Press 1983
* Kettle, Michael *The Allies and the Russian Collapse* Vol.7 Andre Deutsch
* King, Frank H. H. *The Hongkong Bank in Late Imperial China* Cambridge 1987
* Kipfer, A. Historische Wertpapiere der Spanischen Koniglichen und Privaten Handelsgesellschaften des 18. Jahrhunderts.
* * Kuhlmann, Wilhelm, *China's Foreign Debt*
* Lacey, R. *Ford* Guild Publishing 1986
* * Liebig, Michael P. A. *Terra Australis,* Markt & Technik Verlag AG
* *London Encyclopaedia,* Papermac

Mackenzie, C. *Realms of Silver* Routledge & Kegan Paul 1954
May, Robin *The Gold Rushes* William Luscombe 1977
Michie, R. C. *The London & New York Stock Exchanges 1850-1914* Allen & Unwin 1987
Money, D. C. *South America* U.T.P. 1972
Nimmergut, J.*Historische Wertpapiere.* Battenberg, 1991.
Nock, O. S. *World Atlas of Railways*
Norris, W. *The Man Who Fell From the Sky* (Alfred Lowenstein) Viking 1987
Rosenthal, Eric *On 'Change Through the Years — A History of Share Dealing in South Africa'* Flesch Financial Publications 1968
* Schmitz, J. *Historische Wertpapiere das Handbuch fur Sammler und Liebhaber Alter Aktien und Anleihen,* 1982.
* Shakespeare, Howard S. *France — The Royal Loans* Squirrel Publications, 1986
* *Standard Catalogue of World Bonds & Share Certificates, Volume 1, Imperial Russia.* Squirrel Publishing (due early 1995).
London Stock Exchange Official Year Books
Strandberg, B. (and others). *Swedish Share Certifictes before 1850.*
* Suppes. Price guide for Continental European Bonds and Shares.
Swan, Edward J. *Development of the Law of Financial Services* Cavendish Publishing 1993
Wilkinson, D. *Golden Papers.* Perth Westralian Library Foundation 1986
Ziegler, Philip. *The Sixth Great Power — Barings 1762-1929* Collins 1988
Witula, A. *Titoli Azionari ed Obligazioni Antichi,* 1983

In addition, numerous references have been drawn from many well researched auction catalogues, in particular, those of Boone, R M Smythe, Freunde Historischer Wertpapiere, Winslow Associates, M Veissid and Sotheby's.

PUBLICATIONS

Bonds and Shares — Der Wertpapiersammle
Spetzgarterweg 1, 88662 Uberlingen, Germany.
Telepone: 07551-69133   Fax: 07551-65680

Friends of Financial History
26 Broadway (Room 200), New York, NY 10004, USA.
Telepone: 212-908-4519   Fax: 212-908-4600

International Bond and Share Society Journal
6 & 7 Castle Gates, Shrewsbury SY1 2AE, England.
Telepone: 0743-272140   Fax: 0743-366041

INDEX
Page numbers shown in italics refer to illustrations

Accessory Transit Company	135	Brazil Railway Co.	79	Crown United Gold Mining Company	120
Action de Jouissance, definition	51	Brazilian Traction	36	Cunard, Samuel	130
Action de Dividende, definition	51	Bridgewater Canal	134	Daimler-Benz	106, 109
African Steam Ship Company	130	British Honduras Company	135	Daniel Boone	97
African Theatre Company	73	British Australia Gold Mining Co.	117	Dartford Consolidated Tin Mines	120
Age, as affects value	142	Broken Hill Proprietary Company	34	Davis, President Jefferson	28
Akcionarsky Pivovar Na Smichove	149	Brussels Zoo	55, 57	Dawes Loan	53
Alaska	67	Buenos Ayres Tramways Company	77	de Lesseps, Ferdinand	135
Allianz Versicherung AG	46	Buick	108	de Bernales, Claude	34
Amalfi	12	Bull Run, Battle of	28	De Beers	74
American Merchants Union Express Co.	112	Buttonwood Agreement	82	De Dion-Bouton	107
American Bank Note Company	18	Cadillac	109	De La Rue	18
American Express Company	111, 111, 112	Calhoun, John C.	28	Debentures	16
Amsterdam	13, 56	California, State of	84	Decazeville	48
Amsterdam Stock Exchange	13	California King	29	Declaration of American Independence	80
Anglo American Corporation	76	Callao Lima & Oraeja Railway	102	Design	20
Anglo Belgian Patent Flax Wool & Cotton Company	56	Cammel Laird & Co.	130	Detroit & Clleveland Navigation Co.	129
Anglo-Californian Gold Mining Co.	117	Canada	34	Deutsch-Asiatische Bank	38, 53
Annapolis Mining Company	130	Canadian Pacific	35	Deutsche Bank	53
Antwerp	13, 54	Canadian Bank Note Company	18	Deutsche Bundesbank	123
Armavir-Touapse Railway	65	Canal de Richelieu	46	Devon Great Consols Mine	120
Art Deco	23	Canal Maritime de Corinth	135, 136	Direct Drive Motor Company	106
Art Nouveau	23	Canals, background	134	Dodge Autos	109
Atlantic & Pacific Railroad	98	Canton-Kowloon Railway	102, 103	Dolcoath Mine	120
Attractiveness, as affects value	142	Cape of Good Hope Savings Bank	73	Drawn bonds	16
Auctions	140, 148	Cape Town Railway & Dock Co.	73	Drew, Daniel	98
Austin, Stephen F.	27	Cape Town Commercial Exchange	73	Drexel, Anthony	125
Australia	32	Carpathian Bank	125	Drumm and Henseler	8
Australian Agricultural Company	32, 33	Carroll, Charles	97	Durant, William	109
Australian Mining Company	33	Central Pacific RR	98	Dutch East India Company	56
Ave Maria Gold Quartz Mine	117	Charles Pratt & Co.	132	Dutch West India Company	56
Baie Mont St. Michel	49	Charlie Chaplin	36, 110	Early Material	88
Baltic States	68	Chicago and Rock Island RR	98	East India Company (French)	48
Baltimore and Ohio Railway	83, 95, 96, 97	Chicago and Alton	98	East India Company (British)	13
Banana Rio Grande	71	Chilean Northern Railway	19	Edison, Thomas	126
Banco Espanol Del Rio de la Plata	127	China, Bond Settlement	44	Elder Dempster Company	130
Bank of Siberia	122, 124	China, history of	38	Erie Railroad	98, 99
Bank of England	89, 122, 124	Chinese 1913 Reorganisation Loan	40, 41	Ethiopian Railway	18
Bank of the United States	124	Chinese Internal Loans	42	Fargo, William	111
Bank of Charleston	125	City of Vilna	72	Fish, Jim	98
Bank of North America	82, 124	City of Dresden	54	Flagler, Henry	112
Bank of Austalia	33	City of Moscow	65, 68	Ford, Henry	108
Bank of the United States of Pennsylvania	83	City of Riga	72	Framing	145
Bank of New South Wales	33	City of Saratov	65	France	46
Banque Privilegiee & Garantie a Poll & Panheel	53	City of Nicolaiev	67, 68	Franklin, Benjamin	80, 82
Banque Belge	55	City of St. Petersberg	65, 69	Free State of Saxony	54, 55
Bank de Cochinchine	128	City of Kharkov	68	French Rentes	50, 90, 91, 92
Banque Industrielle de Chine	43	City of Baku	65	Fulton, Robert	129
Barcelona Traction Company	36, 37	City of Frankfurt	54	General Motors	109
Barings	83	Claridges	47	General Electric	126
Barnato, Barney	76	Cleveland, Cincinnatti, Chicago & St. Louis Railway	75	Genoa District Waterworks	15
Barnstable Bank	125	Cobalt, Canada	36	Germany	51
BASF	53	Colombia	76	Getty, J. Paul	133
Bau-Gesellschaft fur Eisenbahn-Unternehmungen	50	Colt Gun	61	Gordon-Bennet Cup	107
Baumwoll-Spinnerei Kolbermoor	150	Commercial and Industrial Bank of Russia	124	Gould, Jay	98
Beauregard, General P. G. T.	28	Compagnie des Installations Maritimes de Bruges	2	Grand Trunk Railway of Canada	35
Beech Creek Railroad	101	Compagnie General de Chemins de Fer et de Tramways en Chine	44, 46	Grand Russian Railway Company	66, 67
Beit, Alfred	76	Companhia Nacional de Viacao e Electricidade	25	Great Northern (GB)	60
Belgium	54	Compania Oroya y Mineral de Pasco	74	Great Britain	58
Bernard Hughes Ltd.	143	Companhia de Barcelona	89	Great Western (GB)	60
Biddle, Nicholas	80, 83	Companhia de Navegacao	131	Great Western Railroad of Canada	35
Bingham, William	82	Condition, as affects value	138	Gresham, Sir Thomas	13
Black Sea Kuban Railway	95	Confederate Cotton Bonds	22, 30	Gunder Syndicate Ltd.	72
Bloemfontein Bank	73	Confederate bonds	10, 28, 85	Halifax Banking Company	130
Blue Ridge Railroad Co.	83	Coolgardie	33	Hamilton, Alexander	82, 124
Boston Water Scrip	78	Costa Rica Railway	102, 105	Hargraves, Edward	117
Boxers	38	Creusot	48	Hawaiian Bell Telephone Company	84
Bradbury Wilkinson	18	Crisp Loan 1912	45	Haynes Automobiles	108
				Heraldry	136
				Hispano Suiza	24
				Holland	55
				Hoover, Herbert	33
				Hope Town Diamond Co.	73

156

Hudson River RR Co.	114	National Liberty Bond (China)	43	St. Kilda & Brighton Railway Company	33
Hudsons Bay Company	35	National Bank of the Orange Free State	73	Standard Oil Company	112, *113*
Hughes, John	63	New York Stock Exchange	13, 82	Standard Oil Trust	112
Hukang Railway	*39*, 40	New Jersey Junction Railroad	*126*	Star of Texas	27
Illinois Central Railroad	98	New York & Harlem Railroad	99, *116*	State of Mississippi	10, 94
India General Navigation & Railway Company	87	New Russia Company	63	Stockton and Darlington	59, 94
International Bank (Russia)	124	New York Central Railroad	125	Strand Bridge	*60*
International Railways of Central America	49	New York & Erie Railroad (The 'Erie')	98	Strauss, Johann	114
IOS	*118*	Nicolas Railway	67, 96	Studebaker	108
Jackson, General 'Stonewall'	85	North American Land Company	40, *78*	Sudan Land & Commercial Company	*145*
Jewish Colonial Trust	28, *29*	Northern Inland Navitation Company	135	Suez Canal	135
John Cockerill S A	54	Nurnberg to Furth Railway	51	Syria Ottoman Railway Company	*93*
Kahetian Railway	65	Obligation, definition	51	Thomas, A. Edison	114
Kalgoorlie	33	Oil	133	Thuringia	*52*
Keith, Minor Cooper	102	Oldsmobile	108	Tuolomne County Water Co.	117
Kentucky & Great Eastern Railway	97	Overend & Gurney	*58*	Transfer Certificates, definition	16
Belgium, Kingdom of	*8*	Overland Mail	112	Troitzk Railway	65
Bulgaria, Kingdom of	*11*	Packard	108	Tropical Trading & Transport Company	104
Greece, Kingdom of	*14*	Panama Canal	79, 135	Ukraine	63
Roumania, Kingdom of	*6*	Panhard and Levassor	107	Union Bank (Mississippi)	86
Kokand Namangan Railway	65	Paris France	23	Union Pacific RR	98
Kreuger & Toll	*151*	Paris-Bordeaux-Paris Race (automobiles)	107	United Fruit Company	104
Krupp	53	Part de Fondateur, definition	51	United States of America	80
Kuomintang	40	Peabody, George	125	US Steel Corporation	126
Kursk-Kiev Railway	67	Pearson, F. S.	36, *37*	Vanderbilt, Cornelius	98, 99, 114, 125
Kylsant, Lord	132	Peasants Land Bank	122	Vickers, Son & Maxim Ltd.	110
La Providence	55	Penn Central	100	Volga-Kana Bank	124
La Sautena	*137*	Pennsylvania Railroad Company	100	Warsaw-Vienna Railway	67, 96
Lady Loch Gold Mines	*33*	Pennsylvania Hospital	82	Washington, George	82
Lake Bathurst Australiasian Gold Mining Co.	117	Perkins, Jacob	18	Waterlow (engravers)	18, 40, *41*
Land Bank of the Nobility	122	Perserverance Co.	73	Wells, Henry	111
Law, John	48	Philadelphia & Lancaster Turnpike	79, 82	Wells Fargo Company	111
Le Petit Journal	107	Pierce-Arrow	108	Western Inland Navigation Co.	135
Leipzig-Dresden Railway	51	Pine Creek Railway	*100*	White Star Line	130, *132*
Levis & Kennebec Railway	*35*	Pirie, Lord	132	Whitehead Aircraft	*139*
Library Company of Philadelphia	82	Planters Bank	86	Willing, Thomas	82
Liverpool and Manchester Railway	95	Playboy Enterprises	23, *26*	Willings	82
Lloyd Bank (Hungary)	*20*	Poyais, Kingdom of	78, 113, *115*	Wright, Whittaker	*34*
Locomobile	108	Pratt & Whitney	*140*	Yarmouth Aquarium Society Ltd.	*147*
London and South Africa Exploration Co.	74	Rand Mines Ltd.	76	Yat-sen, Sun	38, 40, *42*
London to Brighton (Race)	107	Rarity	141	Young Loans (Germany)	53
London & Globe	*34*	Rasp, Charles	*34*	Zoos	55, 57
Louisville Bridge Company	*134*	Reischbank	*123*		
Lowenstein, Alfred	36, *37*	Repair and Cleaning	144		
Lung-Tsing-U-Hai Railway	*44*	Repayment of Bounties to Volunteers	27, 28		
Lusitania	36	Republic of Estonia 1927	*70*, 72		
Macgregor, Gregor	78, 113	Rhodes, Cecil	74, 104		
Mackenzie, Sir William	36	Ringling Brothers	*141*		
Mannesmann	53	Robinson, Joseph B.	76		
Marietta & North Georgia Railway	*81*	Rockefeller, John D.	112		
Mary Murphy Gold Mining Company	*119*	Rolls-Royce Ltd.	*22*, *23*		
Mecklenburg-Strelitz road	51	Rothchilds	55		
Medici Bank	54	Royal Mail Steam Packet Co.	132		
Melbourne Suburban Railway Company	*33*	Royal Siamese Government	*21*		
Merchants Union Express Co.	112	Russian Bond Settlement	64		
Mesopotamia	12	Russia	62		
Mestre & Blatge	*107*	Russian Bank for Foreign Trade	122		
Meteor Light & Power	36	Russian Colliery Comapny	*121*		
Mexico	10	Russian Tobacco Company	*17*		
Middlesbrough & Guisbrough Railway	*94*	Salvador Railway	102, *104*		
Mine de Plomb Tenant Argent a Lenards	46	San Antonio Land & Irrigation Company	*36*		
Minerva Motors	107	Santo Domingo company	48		
Mission Development Company	*133*	Schader Coal Mining company	*122*		
Mississippi Company	48	Scrip Certificates, definition	16		
Monti	12	Second Bank of the United States	80, 83		
Monti di Pieta	12	Selma Marion & Memphis Railroad	*177*		
Morgan, J. P.	125	Shanghai-Hangchow-Ningpo Railway	40		
Morris, Robert	79, 80, *82*	Share Warrants, definition	16		
Morris Canal and Banking Co.	125	Siemens	54, *54*		
Mors	107	Simmer & Jack Mines	*73*		
Morse, Samuel	114	Sinking fund	16		
Mucha, Alphonse	23	Societe General	55		
Mudie's Library	*62*	Societe Miniere Intercoloniale	119		
Museum of American Financial History	7	Sons of Gwalia	*34*		
Natal Railway Co.	73	South Africa	72		
		South Sea Company	60, *92*, 93		
		Spanish Trading Companies	88		
		Specimens	*21*, 11, 140		
		Spes Bona Co.	73		